Flying Rocks

Musings of Aviation and Music Adventures

From the zany to scary moments

Michael J. Lofton

FlyingRocksBook.com

Copyright 2024/25 All Rights Reserved

Publishing Copyright and Disclaimer

Copyright @FlyingRocksBook.com 2024/25 - All Rights Reserved

No part of this book may be reproduced or transmitted in any form whatsoever: electronic, or mechanical, including photocopying, recording, or any informational storage, or retrieval system without express written, dated, and signed permission from the author. Once permission is given, the author requires that all such material be cited with the author's name and the title of this book.

Disclaimer and/or Legal Notices
The information presented in this book represents the author's and publisher's views as of the publication date. The author and publisher reserve the right to alter and update content based on new conditions.

This book is for informational and entertainment purposes only. The author and the publisher do not accept any responsibility for any liabilities resulting from using this information. While every attempt has been made to verify the information provided herein, the author and the publisher cannot assume any responsibility for errors, inaccuracies, or omissions. The content is simply the author's remembered experiences. Sometimes, first names might have been used if they were still alive. Full names were used if they died or otherwise with approval. None of the band names are fictional.

Images: All images and text are owned by the author. Interested parties must retain permission for reprinting or distribution. Once permission is given, the author requires that all images and text be cited with the author's name and the title of this book. For the record, the mention of this book was originally documented on the personal Author's Blog site starting in the year 2013.

- Author's Blog: https://michaellofton.com/
- Facebook: https://www.facebook.com/61565620089833

Contact source for permissions
c/o Michael J Lofton
michael@customercounts.com
Customer Counts Publishing and Marketing
ISBN #979-8-218-58063-6

Citations and References

Throughout this book I made an effort to provide citations and references to certain subject matters via a QR code, linking to an appropriate landing page that best describes such mentions in the chapters.

For the risk of being criticized for placing these references throughout the content copy, I've embarked on a different approach to such citation positioning. Not necessarily at the bottom of the page, but throughout the read... Screw tradition.

However after saying that, I place citation references at the bottom of some chapters. This approach to referencing such material allows you to grab your cell phone and scan the QR code to supplement your physical book reading. If you're already viewing this book via your cell phone, laptop, or desktop, the clickable reference anchor link will also open in a separate tab to the same location as the QR code.

Note: In older editions of this book the QR codes may have been changed in order to re-direct to updated reference locations as required. In such instances, the associated anchor-links may differ.

Air Note and Flashback

Air Note refers to certain subject citation matters mentioned within chapters.

- Subject Matter -

https://URL of QR code with anchor link
(sometimes an image is included in the Air Note)

Flashback describes my recall of a related subject matter mentioned.

Description of Flashback... *Sometimes a QR code with an anchor link is included.*

* * *

These citations lead off in many directions. YouTube, Blogs, Social Media, Web references, including WIKI. it's understood that WIKI can have some aberrations within descriptions, yet I attempt to use such only for the most basic background references.

Except for an initial AI (Artificial Intelligence) prompt in creating part of the cover image design, along with just a few of the small illustrative icons, and for the Air Note and Flashback icons, all art plagiarism was verified as original in designs.

This book's content text was not written with any assistance from AI. It's otherwise 100 percent organic by the author. All photographic images are from the Author's library of past photos. The text content is a written reflection of real-life 'analog' experiences. It might even be one of the last non-AI text-influenced books you might ever read. LOL, let's hope it hasn't gone that far, eh?

Please report any broken links or QR codes to...
michael@customercounts.com

Preface and Dedication
Rogue Musings and Tales of a Rock n' Roll Pilot

It was 1959 and Disneyland in Southern California had recently opened. This is where I was exposed to the concept of lift as my first introduction to flight. The theme park's premier ride was a whirling spaceship located in Tomorrowland. I was all of 7 years old.

Example of Rocket Ride

As a young boy, the ride looked rather menacing. Despite my youthful sense of trepidation, I must have indicated a faint interest, as my father convinced me to hop aboard.

First, it spun around at ground level, then it lifted to an altitude of a good 20 feet (LOL)! However, that twirling flight level felt more like a thousand feet and scared the fuckin' pants off of me (ok, I didn't know how to swear then). I could hardly wait for the ride to be over.

As soon as I stepped off that spaceship, I wiped the tears of terror from my eyes as I finally felt a sigh of relief. Yet a sense of accomplishment remained even with my being a wimp.

The importance of this spaceship ride experience would expose itself again later in my youth with a more invigorating and delightful outcome.

My next flight milestone came in my mid-teens. This time learning to fly in a Cessna 170 tail-dragger airplane that replaced the whirling spaceship ride. The added elements of controlling my ship in the air, including a perpetual change of scenery and the ability to stop the flight by the pilot's choice, were exhilarating.

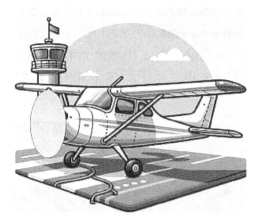

Cessna 170 (example)

This book not only delves into my personal experiences flying and arranging private air transportation of some of the most famous and influential musical entertainers of the world, but it also touches upon the lives of rockers who had met their demise in private aircraft... Not to be morbid, you'll discover more about what I mean as you read on.

This publication doesn't necessarily dive into the personal lives of famous entertainers, there may be some hints but if you're looking for heavy star gossip crap, it's not in this book. It's an insider's backstage production look at how the private air transportation portion of entertainment touring works... It's about what gets them to their stage to perform. The production back side of the aviation biz, as it related (back then) to my flying big-time entertainers.

If you're intrigued by airplanes, famous musicians, or just some wacky interesting stories that relate to what happens backstage with music and aviation, this read might be for you.

For the socially-minded person, private aircraft transportation might seem pretentious. Many entertainers have determined private aircraft excel over commercial airline travel. Flying in and out of arrival and departure airports closer to the venues, without fan pressures and airline delays. The private airplane has earned its place in the entertainment touring industry as a valid, essential transportation tool.

I realize that I'm not a professional storyteller. Heck, you'll even see some professional edits slide to retain my way of wording. After enough edits (omg) it was finally time to get some of my (his) stories off my computer and off to print. I've somewhat attempted to set the chapter flow in the sequence of my flying life at that time. It starts and ends with my first client, Jimmy Buffett.

The bottom line is that I feel so privileged to have flown and arranged private air transportation for the biggest and the best of major rock 'n roll bands, along with other VIPs, in those great days gone by. Still diggin' my life at this point with my continued present moments, albeit not in the aviation biz anymore.

Somehow I literally fell into almost all of my past flying and aircraft maintenance gigs that allowed me to support and raise my family along the way.

Speaking of family during those interesting years, I fully dedicate this book to my, ex-wife Sunshine, mother of our two children, Fawn and Ethan. Our children Rock! Much Love Going Out to You, along with my Grandkids (as of this early edition), Xander, Brooklyn, and Cole.

Love You! - Dad/G-Pa

Foreword

As a child growing up my parents owned a private airplane. I remember thinking it was the norm to own a Cessna 421 twin-engine plane. My Dad was a pilot, a flight instructor, and an aviation technician/Inspector. He owned an aviation business, flying rock stars around North America. My Mom almost gave birth to me on our plane as my Dad flew her to the hospital while she was in labor.

Flying in our own personal 7-passenger plane instead of driving to my grandparent's house for long weekend visits. Hanging out at the airport, playing hide and seek in the airplane hangers my Dad built, and riding my bike on the airplane runway in our small Colorado town. All seemed normal and fun.

Our home hallway walls were decorated with hanging autographed album covers, golden records, and photos of my Dad and his "buddy" Jimmy Buffet. This was what I considered a normal childhood. It wasn't until I would tell or show my friends our plane, that they would respond with wide eyes, "Your family owns a plane?!"

Come to quickly find out my childhood was not the norm. At that time, Gold Mountain Aviation and Intercharter were his companies.

One of my most vivid memories of my Dad's air charter business was on August 9, 1995. Our house phone rang and my Dad picked up the call. I could tell from the look on his face something was wrong. He hung up the phone and was crying. I had never seen my Dad cry before that moment. I started to panic asking him if something happened to Mom. He looked up and said, "Jerry's dead!" as he continued to cry. He was referring to the one and only Jerry Garcia. At that time, the Grateful Dead was a client of his, and he was one of the first people to get the call right after Jerry had passed.

One of the biggest things I have personally learned from my Dad is to always dream big. My Dad wanted to be more than just a pilot. He was always passionate about rock n roll as he was a musician himself. Dreaming big, he combined both of his passions in life and created something bigger, something magical, something legendary.

Love,
Fawn (Daughter) "Strong Mind, Strong Body, Strong Soul"

My Dad's Favorite Pic of Me
Heading out to my first day of School

Hey Dad!
So, since it was near the end of your aviation career, I only remember a little when you were flying or being on tour. Mostly what I remember is the tour/band memorabilia, and the music studio in the basement at the Mesa house in Durango, Colorado.
One fun memory is building forts in the basement using blankets and microphone/music stands, playing the sound system on the big stage monitors, and the funky cool lighting.

I also remember the home office and visiting you at the office in town for your flying magazine. So, for me, it was more of a secondhand experience—playing with the audio gear and drums, looking at the tour photos, and the aircraft photos on the wall with Jimmy Buffet, Grateful Dead, Heart, Van Halen, etc.

I do remember you taking me out to the airport when that occasional entertainment plane of yours would arrive at Durango. I recall me sitting in Dwight Yoakam's Gulfstream. Do you still have those pictures?

Love,
Ethan (Son)

Fawn, with Ethan, along with his friend, and the pilot of Dwight Yoakam's aircraft

Ethan in Dwight's aircraft with his friend

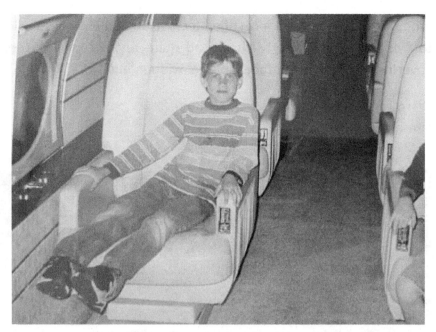

Ethan hanging out in style

Back in the day before I met Michael, I was a bit down on corporate anything. That all changed when I witnessed the way Michael navigated the business terrain. His entrepreneurial sense directed him to be professional with clients and also very creative and humanistic. His calm casual approach connected him to people in a way where they put their trust in his decisions and actions.

I found that some of the types of aircraft that Michael articulately flew were like hotels on wheels. He worked hard in this eclectic industry managing and adhering to the many different personalities of his entertainer clients.

Michael was an efficient and safe pilot. I will always remember wanting to have a home birth with our daughter, Fawn. After being in labor for an extensive amount of time, Michael flew me and one of our midwives down the mountain to get to a hospital. Fawn could have been born in the aircraft! We enjoyed having a small plane to go short distances with our daughter and son. Often, our dog Sky was our co-pilot!

Michael had a close relationship with Jimmy Buffet and his road manager Bobby. I love that Jimmy put full faith in Michael to give him some flying lessons.

From fixing airplanes as a certified technician and flight instructor to flying the big stars, Michael had quite an extensive career, covering many different facets of the aviation industry.

Warmly,
Sunshine

*Sunshine, ex-wife and mother of Fawn and Ethan,
on the flight deck of the Fleetwood-Mac Tusk Boeing bird.*

Past Flight Clients

Jimmy Buffett and the Coral Reefers
- 13 years ('78 - '91)
Heart - 13 years (80s - early 90s)
Grateful Dead Band - and last to fly Jerry Garcia
- 17 years (late 70s - till Jerry died - '95)
Jerry Garcia Band - 10 years (80s - early 90s)
Van Halen w Sammy Hagar years and VH III tour
- 7 years ('91 - '98)
Barry Manilow - 5 years (90s)
Tim Allen
Quincy Jones
Huey Lewis
Doobie Brothers - Reunion Tour - '87
Osmonds Brothers - Sold them a Westwind 1123 Aircraft
Rolling Stones Steel Wheels Tour - ('89 - '90)
Jefferson Starship
Crystal Gayle
Rod Stewart
Anita Baker
Garrison Keiller – NPR Radio hour with Chet Atkins tour
Jerry Brown - CA. Governor & Heads of State
Guns N Roses BFD 'Riot' Tour - ('91 - '92)
LeAnn Rimes
Dionne Warwick
Kenny Loggins
Kings of Comedy Film Tour
Englebert Humperdink
Ozzy Osbourne
Duran Duran
Paul Simon Born at the Right Time Tour - ('90 - '91)
Richard Marx - World Record Tour - ('91)
Meatloaf – Bat Out Of Hell II – Back into Hell tour
Commodores with Lionel Ritchie - ('77)
Lou Rawls - ('77)
Elvis Presly (almost) – ('77)

Flying Rocks
Table of Contents

Entry Splash Page
Publishing Copyright and Disclaimer
Citations and References
Preface and Dedication
Foreword
Past Flight Clients

Chapters
1. Jimmy Buffett meets Lynard Skynard in flight, part one / Pg 1
2. Lionel Richie and the Commodores Brick House Tour / Pg 9
3. The Original Cheeseburger Airplane - JB logo / Pg 21
4. Grateful Dead - Long Strange Lovely Trips / Pg 51
5. Ricky 'Rick' Nelson / Pg 59
6. Barry Manilow / Pg 67
7. Nazareth - Lightening, Smoke, and the Border Crossings / Pg 75
8. Osmond Brothers Jet / Pg 99
9. Grateful Dead – Banks Won't Fly Them / Pg 113
10. Richard Marx - World Record / Pg 121
11. Jimmy Buffett - Viscount Tour / Pg 123
12. Backstage, Insights, and Other Shenanigans / Pg 129
13. Dan Fogelberg / Pg 137
14. Other Entertainers Flown (without deep stories) / Pg 141
15. Heads of State and VIPs (Suits) / Pg 157
16. Heart / Pg 163
17. Jimmy Buffett – Volcano Blew Again / Pg 173
18. Doobie Brothers – Reunion Tour / Pg 183
19. Rolling Stones – Steel Wheels Tour / Pg 197
20. Van Halen / Hagar Years + VH-III / Pg 207
21. Guns N' Roses - Riot Tour / Pg 217
22. Grateful Dead – Cocaine and Wine & Final Show CHG / Pg 227
23. Jimmy Buffett Meets Skynard in-flight, conclusion / Pg 235

Bio - Outro - Acknowledgments

A Brush With The Other Side
Jimmy Buffett Meets Lynyrd Skynyrd Inflight?
- Mystery Unforeseen Part One -

"Looking out my right side cockpit window I witnessed sparks flying out from the front of our right-hand #2 engine... Lots of bright flashing sparks! WTF!?"

As quoted from Wikipedia... "Following a performance at the Greenville Memorial Auditorium in Greenville, South Carolina, on October 20, 1977, the Lynyrd Skynyrd band boarded a chartered Convair CV-240 airplane bound for Baton Rouge, Louisiana, where they were scheduled to appear at LSU the following night."

Due to a faulty engine situation during their flight, the Skynyrd aircraft ran low on fuel and their pilots diverted to the nearby McComb-Pike County Airport. Their aircraft never made it to that location. You no doubt know that many on board perished that day. Very unfortunate!

It mentioned a faulty engine. Understanding that airplane engines have their issues for sure, most in-flight discrepancies (noted in the aviation industry as Squawks) can be ascertained and dealt with to secure a safe landing. However, in this instance, running out of fuel due to a faulty fuel system, the Skynyrd flight crew attempted an emergency landing. Yet instead, they crashed into a heavily forested area five miles northeast of Gillsburg, Mississippi.

Totally sucks!

Considering the pilots had time to rectify the situation and otherwise get the aircraft on the ground sooner and safely, the crew decided to stretch their luck, to no avail.

Lynyrd Skynyrd Convair CV-240 Crash

https://flyingrocksbook.com/pHX

So, what does Lynyrd Skynyrd have to do with me and my aviation adventures flying and securing private aircraft for rock stars in the 70s, 80s, and 90s?... And for that matter, specifically in this instance with Jimmy Buffett?

Well, less than six months after the Skynyrd airplane crash, I delivered an Fairchild f-27 Turbo-Prop aircraft to the mid-west to pick up Jimmy Buffett and his Coral Reefer band, for what would eventually be a couple of years of touring as their pilot.

After a couple of years on the road with Jimmy and his Coral Reefer band, this particular flight was at the very end of Buffett's late-70s Summer tours. This would be my last flight as his personal pilot before I went on to remain as their private air transportation consultant for another ten years.

The original Jimmy Buffett Cheeseburger Airplane - Fairchild F27

At this point, we were flying the Fairchild F-27, aka the original "Cheeseburger" airplane — a twin-engine turboprop high-winged craft. The ship required two pilots, a captain, and co-captain positions. For a couple of years up to this point, both myself (mostly flying as co-captain duties) and my hired captain, William, had already been piloting Jimmy and the Coral Reefer Band on all of their '78 & '79 tours.

It was sometime late in '79, when we were on our final legs of Buffett's tours for that year. I can't totally remember (imagine, at my age) but it was a one-off late evening flight after a gig from either, going to or from, the Shreveport, LA or Jackson, MS area. Our flight took us over a certain, particular location. More on where later in this chapter.

The usual entourage was on board, Jimmy and the Coral Reefer Band. Come to think of it, we might have had a member or two from an opening act.

A short bit into our flight, we could see some very large thunderstorms scattered to the southeast, reaching out over the Gulf of Mexico. Lucky for us they were not a part of our flight route.

An incredible continuous display of flash lightning exploded in the sky that late evening flight, not unlike the display at a Boston Pops celebration on the fourth of July. It was a very intense visual performance. From an altitude you really appreciate a new view of Mother Nature.

We had managed to stay clear of most of the weather activity at a flight level averaging 25,000 feet (Flight Level 250). Flying mostly in and above light AltoCumulus cloud layers with light chop (turbulence). At twenty-five thou, it's damn cold outside!

AltoCumulus Cloud Layers

https://flyingrocksbook.com/i52

3

There's an old saying in aviation that states, "A pilot's duties during flights are mostly routine observations, except for the very occasional shear chaos situations."

On this, my final JB flight as his personal pilot, everything seemed straightforward. All systems were stable and the flight route remained as planned.

All of a sudden, within the time frame of a few seconds, our autopilot clicked off, then back on, then off again. Captain Bill and I both reached for the Yoke (the flight wheel) to secure and maintain the stability of our craft.

Since the captain was in the left seat on this leg, William had final control and called out, "I've got the ship." I immediately acknowledged his taking command of the flight controls and released my grip on the Yoke. Protocol on the flight deck has its hierarchy.

At the same time that our autopilot acted up, most of our lights on the flight deck began to dim and flicker. The captain and I casually looked at each other, remarking at the same time... "What the fuck!?" (later known as WTF in the digital world (hehe))

Staying calm over the matter, we further pondered.

It seemed a strange event but if you've been flying an aircraft for many years circumstances arise from time to time that demand your deeper attention than normal routine flights. In this instance, we figured that with all the electrical (lightning) activity that evening, maybe a St Elmo's fire condition was taking place as a temporary explanation.

St. Elmo's Fire

https://flyingrocksbook.com/gKN

After a few moments had passed, our situation seemed to normalize and the aircraft electronics returned to what appeared to be standard flight conditions.

Captain Bill called out... "let's try to reset the autopilot again." So, I reached over and called out, "autopilot setting to the on position," with the cap's response, "Confirmed." With a two-pilot craft, you always double-check each other with a follow-up voice verification.

The Cheeseburger Fairchild once again was tracking on our course heading and holding our assigned altitude.

A good few minutes passed and all seemed fine. We found ourselves somewhat comfortable, monitoring our stabilized flight instruments.

Then it happened again!

The lights in the flight deck started to flicker. Once again the autopilot clicked off... Captain William called out, "I've got the ship!"

This time we both acknowledge that we had a more serious situation at hand.

In any emergency or unusual flight conditions the very first thing a pilot, or in our case a flight crew will do, is to make sure that the aircraft is secured in a stable flight condition. In this instance, the captain was manually handling the ship, straight and level.

No matter what, you always control and fly your aircraft first.

Our situation now demanded some special attention. And it wasn't long before our attention became a touch more intense.

Just then, Bobby, Jimmy's road manager, opens the flight deck (cockpit) door and says, "Hey guys, the lights back in the cabin are flashing on and off."

I looked over at Bobby and told him that we were experiencing a strange circumstance and needed to concentrate on the task at hand. I asked that he return to the cabin and explain to Jimmy and the folks in the back that we were indeed working on the situation.

Just then, a tremendous amount of light emitted from my right-hand starboard windscreen!

Starboard and Port

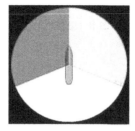

https://flyingrocksbook.com/9In

I looked out my starboard side and witnessed sparks flying out from the front of our (right-hand) #2 engine... Lots of bright, flying sparks!

Not something one looks forward to during their flying career!

My first impression was that it appeared to be a turbine blade rubbing with subsequent metal-to-metal friction, provoking sparking.

Being a very rare event, turbine blade(s) rubbing can be a very unpleasant scenario. Structural damage to an engine could be catastrophic. Furthermore, in monetary terms, uh, very painful!

So, the captain gently yet strongly states, "Well, that doesn't look very good from my point of view, what the heck is happening over there, Lofton?" I go, "Hold on, still observing the status."

Being in the captain's (left) seat, William could not see our starboard engine. So it was required that the co-pilot [me] pass along any updates from my direct point of view.

Sparks from this part of the Nacelle's heated inlet.

I immediately looked back and scanned our engine gauges to see if any aberrations were immediately present. All of our flight panel instruments still looked good. Once the autopilot had clicked off, all other indications and lights stabilized.

I asked the Cap if he noticed any unusual indications on our panel. He mentioned that all looked good, except for our 'B' electrical bus (distribution of electric loads), which was indicating 'off'. It clicked off at the same time we lost our autopilot, the second time.

The 'B' panel was the same electrical bus provided for by the right engine's generator. It made sense the discrepancy was indeed coming from our right engine sparking scenario. Now we are trying to figure out just why!

The sparks continued to fly... A gigantic exploding sparkler... A big-ass sparkler!

We definitely had a right-side engine condition, but what the hell was it?

At this point, we were both prepared and ready to shut this engine down if needed. We were trained to handle almost any situation and yes, this twin-engine machine would have flown just fine with only one other turbine engine turning.

The captain called out to me, "Michael, it's your call, what's it going to be, are we shutting down that engine?"

Captain Bill had his hand at the lever ready to cut the fuel off to that engine. Subsequently, we would feather the propeller to reduce drag once the engine was shuttered.

Feathering a propeller and why (due to drag)

https://flyingrocksbook.com/qVM

It was indeed decision time, since if it were an engine turbine blade rubbing condition we couldn't risk further engine damage, as well as a possible in-flight fire, by any means. Yet again, we hadn't experienced any vibration which would have indicated an engine rubbing condition.

Even though we had continuous stable engine output read-out conditions, we needed to decide soon.

I called out to the captain... "Let me take one more good hard look and we'll make our final decision momentarily." he responded, "Your call, Michael."

This time I specifically visually honed in on our engine and concentrated on where the immense amount of sparks emitted...

At this point in the story, I pick up the final events of this flight and how it relates to Lynyrd Skynyrd, at the end of the book. OK, maybe I'm teasing you a little. If you wish, hop to the end to finish this read... And/or, in the meantime, how about we venture on...

The Commodores

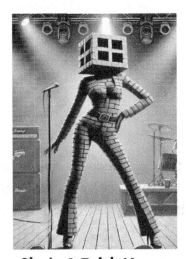

She's A Brick House

White Boys Backstage Dodging Flying Bottles

Back in 1977 the Commodores, when Lionel Richie (aka: he was then called: Skeeter) was their lead singer, I was co-pilot (second in command) on their North American Brick House Tour.

Personal Signed Album by the Commodores

Commodores

https://flyingrocksbook.com/qW5

I hadn't heard of the Commodores up to that point in my life. I know, rather lame on my part for sure. It happened to be one of their last tours with Skeeter, just before Richie headed out on his solo career.

The band did have some popular songs that became hits. I liked 'Zoom'... The tune was mesmerizing when they played it live.

Zoom... Zoom, Zoom (the song performed live)

https://flyingrocksbook.com/aMW

Like most bands, the Commodores were a wonderful group of entertainers to fly. Always chuckin' and Jivin' with jokes and totally fun to be around.

During many of our flight legs, most of the band members (including Lionel Richie) would venture up to the flight deck and discuss aviation and the music industry, along with other topics that came up that day.

This Brick House Tour was filling thirty thousand (plus) stadium seats nightly... it was a monster tour!

The aircraft provided for this venture was a Viscount 700 series ship in an executive configuration.

Viscount Aircraft History

https://flyingrocksbook.com/pK2

Not being a very fast aircraft, pushing it, the Viscount could maybe reach an average cruising speed of approximately 250+ knots - around 285 mph - at a flight level of no higher than an average of twenty-eight thousand feet (eg., Flight Level 280)

The Viscount aircraft was designed as a short-haul airliner, so there was no need for high speeds or altitudes. However, during my time flying on this plane, it would have been beneficial to fly at higher levels to avoid weather patterns on longer flights. Check out the chapter about flying the Nazareth Band Crew.

A few times, but not a lot, we pilots would take turns venturing back to the passenger cabin to check in on things. Generally, it was more of a comfort visit. Whereby, I might ask a few band members or road management if everything seemed ok with their ride. Questions like; how's the cabin temperature for everyone, or was there anything about the food or cabin amenities they'd like to change.

We respected their privacy. Mostly, our occasional visit with the passengers was to simply say hello and ask how things were going. We'd check to see if any safety issues might be present. Yet, for the most part, our stay in the cabin area was limited, since our position was to be flying the aircraft, not hanging out with the band (fgs).

Interior of Viscount

During the time era when the Viscount and other similar-sized aircraft, such as the Fairchild F27, Convairs, and Lockheeds, were in use, touring artists found them to be a great option for accommodating their large entourage of 15 to 20 passengers with executive-style seating. In their original airline configuration, they typically had all-forward-facing seats up to 60 people for commercial operations. These custom aircraft had an enormous interior with comfortable living-room-style seating arrangements.

I've been asked many times what it was like flying famous music stars. All the glamour of just hanging out with them.

Well, there was a bit of favoritism that came with the territory of being their pilots. But my main reference to my responsibilities was always the directive to get our passengers to their destination safely.

The star struck thing never really reached into my mind. Once I got to know our entourage, I soon discovered how down-to-earth these peeps were. Of course the private airplane scene enhanced their presence, but the group (like most all of my clients) themselves remained humble and in-the-moment with real conversations.

Lionel on the Viscount Steps

Most of the flights only included band members, their wives, or girlfriends, along with any essential stage crew members. Rarely would you see a groupie within this environment. It would be a very rare occasion indeed since the aircraft was considered a sacred space. An escape capsule of sorts, well away from their fans.

Almost all of the flights on the Brick House tour departed early in the afternoon for what were a maximum of a couple of en-route flight hours, or within a few hundred miles. This way the ground crew could transport all of the band's equipment by ground, and be set up in the next city before we arrived that afternoon for sound check.

On our last leg of this Brick House Tour, heading back to the Commodores' town, Tuskegee, AL., Lionel 'Skeeter' joined us on the flight deck shortly after departure that evening and invited us to stop by his home the very next day to relax and discuss some post-tour reflections.

The next afternoon Lionel and his wife (at that time) offered up some great snacks and drinks and during our short stay at their home, Richie sat behind his grand piano and sang a couple of songs that he mentioned he was developing. One of the songs was later released on his solo album after his departure from the Commodores, called, Truly.

Lionel Richie, Truly

https://flyingrocksbook.com/iaZ

While we were at Skeeter's house, listening to him laying down his tunes, hanging with the captain and our flight attendant, I reflected on the Tuskegee Airmen. They were created just down the street from Lionel's home.

Being a pilot and part-time musician, I was always on the lookout for any associated flight and music references during my time flying entertainers on the road.

We learned that Richie grew up on the campus of the Tuskegee Institute where he also accepted a tennis scholarship.

Tuskegee Airmen

https://flyingrocksbook.com/NQi

What a great trip!

White Boys Backstage...

One of our stops on this 1977 tour included the New Orleans Super Dome.

Backstage at the Super Dome was a bit different than that of a smaller, dedicated music venue. For example, the stage was in the in-zone of the football stadium, and as such, the back staging area was somewhat open to the public eyes, but not accessible. The dressing rooms and catering were mostly closed-in, yet, the general backstage area was exposed to some of their fans.

Our crew consisted of myself, the co-pilot, a white guy. The caption of the aircraft, a white guy, and our flight attendant, a (very cute) white girl. Essentially, we were (pretty much) the only white folk at this concert of many thousand of peeps!

While negotiating our way to the backstage area, a loud crash of glass close to us became apparent. I shouted out to the Commodores tour manager. "What the Hell was that?" His response was, "It was a beer bottle, and they're going to be throwing a lot more of that kind of shit at you guys, so keep your eyes open and your heads down."

Mind you, these were beer bottles not cans being tossed in our direction.

I said something kinda [really] stupid like, "Do you think it has to do with us being some of the only white folk in the Super Dome, with close to 50 thousand plus fans?" The road manager simply turns to me and says, "No shit, you think?!" (ha!)

A few more bottles continued to be hurled and breaking around us!

Finally, the road manager goes, "Dudes, for your safety, you white brothers just might want to venture into the dressing rooms away from viewing eyes... Nothing against you, and don't take offense, but it's a racially sensitive scene here and I'm sure you guys no doubt were expecting a bit of this kind of excitement."

Indeed we were aware of what might develop regarding this scenario.

Anyway, the road manager goes on to say, "Look, we'll be needing you as a healthy flight crew for our next flight, so stay low dudes." As he chuckled. We all had a burst of understood laughter.

Now this was the 70s and I had grown up around a racially mixed high school in Los Angeles, back in the original Watts riot days.

I've been around the block with my share of racial tussles, and I totally got the Super Dome scene.

I'm talking about the original Watts riot in the late 60's btw, not the subsequent 90's episode. I witnessed Watts burning from my Southern California high school campus, John Muir High, in Pasadena, California. Since the campus was only a handful of miles from the heart of that smoky Los Angeles scene.

We had campus clashes all the time between different colors... White, Black, Hispanic, Asian... and, I pretty much understood what was up and worked my way through it all.

Can't believe the racial shit is still going on over a half-century later (as I finish the first edition of this book in 2024)... Jeez, let's get over it already. WTF? Can you say gov't propaganda, perpetuating their agenda to keep us against one another? (IMHO)

Anyway, we ended up back at the dressing rooms of the Super Dome where we grabbed some catering grub and hung out with the touring crew reflecting on the scene and generally peeking out the backstage doorway every once in a while to view and enjoy a bit of the Commodores concert performance.

After the gig, we (the flight crew) were escorted, along with the band, to limos for our route (escape) back to our hotel.

Great backstage experiences came in many forms, and this was an interesting reflection, for sure! LOL!

Author/Pilot on Commodores Viscount aircraft

The Brick House Women Selection Committee!

As I mentioned, the Commodores guys were a trip to hang out with. During their show, when their 'Brick House Woman' song was introduced and played, numerous and willing ladies danced across the stage in bikini attire. The band and/or stage crew members hand-picked each brick house lady before each of their shows.

Commodores - Brick House

https://flyingrocksbook.com/aci

One day, well before I left my hotel to gather for some backstage catering at that night's concert, Skeeter (Lionel) knocked on my hotel door. Band member, Walter, might have also been with him. He goes, "How would you like to be on the selection committee to determine which brick house women will be dancing across our stage tonight?" I looked at Skeeter and without hesitation, cheerfully responded, "OK, Sure!" (hehe)

Skeeter goes, "Great, so here's what you do." He goes on to explain the criteria for selection. "We allow around four women to qualify, yet you'll have well over that many showing up at your hotel room door to attempt to qualify."

Richie continued, "The mission of the ladies is to show off their bodies and 'verbally' convenience you as to why they like the Commodores, and in as few words as possible, why they should be selected to be a 'Brick House Woman' for this night's stage walk."

Off to work I go. (hehe, haha!)

Within a half-hour of my assignment, the first door knock happened. It was a pair of ladies, sisters no less. They go, "We heard that you fine white boy is part of picking the Brick House winners tonight." Stumbling for a reasonable answer, I lamely go, "Yes, I'm on the committee."

Both of them were wearing full-length fur coats. I'd soon discover that most of the potential contestants dawned full-length Fur coats. Some wore leather swimsuits.

Of note, Lionel further suggested that I never invite the brick house contestants inside the hotel room. Since many other eligible ladies would soon be knocking, it was best to simply judge, gather their names, verify their contact, and then have them immediately move along. I remained a very good (oh brother!) pilot.

Those sisters, along with the other entries, were there to show off their bodies, to attempt to obtain the winner edge/nod and go-ahead, to access the stage that eve.

Upon the opening of their coats, the lack of any bikini attire was very apparent. "Oh, Wow you ladies are very endowed" were my lame words. They both looked and laughed. "Honey", they explained to me (even though I already knew this) "the bikini would be worn as a requirement for the song and stage strut across the stage that eve, but wanted to make a statement." Oh man, they did ever!

Anyway, it was pretty much like this for almost another hour. The bottom line, it was very hard to pick just a few! (OMG-LOL!). Somehow I put a final list together, passed it on to the production staff, and then it was off to the venue to indulge in some catered dinner and a drink to 'cool me off' a bit!

The Brick House tour will be well remembered... LOL!

Firecrackers Under My Hotel Door!

As part of the experience of flying tours (like this), our crew, similar to that of the band and their crew members, would pull shenanigans on each other.

One of the evenings in my hotel on this tour, while in a deep sleep, I was awakened by the loud banging sounds of gunshots being fired inside my room... WTF!

As part of a crew gag, my Captain of the ship decided that now would be a good time to perform a gag by sliding a string of firecrackers under my hotel door at 2 am. Shook the shit out of me!

All this came with the territory of being on a music tour. LOL. It was my turn to experience a prank!

BTW... Regarding the history of the Viscount aircraft and Rock n' Roll... Take a peek at the book written by one of the most prominent stewardesses who flew with many of the legendary rock bands of the late 20th century, Go Enterprise in Burbank, California... Linda Laidlaw, called: Coffee, Tea and Rock 'n' Roll.

An interview with Linda can be heard here: FlyingRocksBook.com *(check under Audio Interviews tab)*

 **My Original Facebook posting (dated 2013)**
https://flyingrocksbook.com/HPr

The Original Cheeseburger Airplane
'You Had To Be There'

I Was There!

Original Cheeseburger F27 Airplane (early brochure cover)

It was late winter of 1977 when, from what appeared out of the (Bubbles-Up!) blue, I received a phone call from a travel agent who mentioned he had a client who needed an aircraft for an entertainment tour. This agent asked if I could do this kind of work.

I thought to myself at that time (remembering while I was fairly young), why not set up an aircraft flight service consultation company and fly entertainers myself?

Along with no doubt a decent spark from the universe, my name had come up in a circle of associates that I was flying entertainers with Go Enterprise, a major entertainment private travel service in Burbank, California. I also managed my personal operations on the side. A charter company flying fishermen in twin-engine aircraft from Southern California into Baja Mexico, while also maintaining as a mechanic, two flying school airplane flight lines.

Not sure where that spark came from but anyway, the agent then mentioned that the client interested in an aircraft for touring was a singer-songwriter named, Jimmy Buffett.

"Jimmy who?" was my remark. I hadn't heard of Jimmy Buffett to this point.

Jimmy's seat was always first chair facing forward on the port side

 It was the summer of '77 at a gathering with friends for BBQ and general hang time in my Southern California [Crestline] mountain neighborhood. I noticed numerous peeps at that party were singing the lyrics to the background radio music of the song Margaritaville.

Within six months after that, I would (of all things) be arranging and flying Jimmy's, Son of A Son of A Sailor, and Cheeseburger In Paradise tours. I would then continue as his personal flight consultant for ten years thereafter... Ha! What a trip!

BTW, since Jimmy was one of the first entertainers that I flew under my aviation consultation business, you'll no doubt notice a slight bias in this publication, along with the Grateful Dead.

Son of a Son of A Sailor

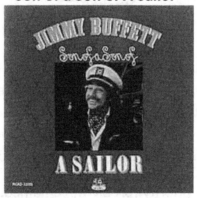

https://flyingrocksbook.com/fgk

As interesting as this opportunity seemed to fly Jimmy Buffett, a few immediate caveats laid in front of me. I had no aircraft to handle the likes of flying Jimmy and his band on tour, and I hadn't any idea where I would secure such an aircraft, nor the financing. Heck, I might of had just enough money at that time to pay my next month living expenses, along with some food to get me by for a week. LOL!

Yet, for some reason, my young rebel soul blood was suggesting to Buffett's representative agent that I could indeed pull this off!... Oh boy, there I was, just 25 years of age and stepping a touch (maybe way) out of my league. But I felt ready for the venture.

A large aircraft was required for the Buffett tours, because it needed to carry an average of 12 - 15 passengers. My experience with Go Enterprise as a sub-contracted pilot/mechanic for their fleet of Viscount aircraft suggested that I didn't want to support a 4-engine machine. However, the Rolls Royce turboprop engines that propelled that aircraft did prove to be a reliable and excellent choice of powerplant. Now the question was, which aircraft would it be, and how in the world would I secure such a craft?

Rolls Royce Dart 510 Turbo Prop Engine

https://flyingrocksbook.com/SoA

What I've subsequently termed, 'synchronicity' (aka, manifestation alignment - wtf you say?), after some initial research, I stumbled across an aircraft for sale located in the Minneapolis MN area. It was owned by a local TV Station, the Hubbard TV Broadcasting Company. A Fairchild F-27 twin-engine turboprop.

Only one (major) priority [problem] remained... no money to buy this or any other possible aircraft to fulfill Buffett's tour request.

OK, I was indeed 'winging it!' Something was nudging me on.

Immediately thereafter, another synchronistic event presented itself. Within days of stumbling upon the F-27, and to this day I have no idea why this event happened (hello universe!), I received a phone call from an individual seeking an investment in an aircraft. He was looking for a tax write-off, as airplanes at that time (even today I believe) offered a great accelerated tax write-off alternative. We're talking about 3 - 5 years acellerated. I remember almost choking on my coffee that morning of that investor's call. At first, I thought maybe he wanted a smaller airplane, then it hit me to ask if a larger investment (eg., the Fairchild) with a lease-back management arrangement with me for some upcoming Buffett tours would interest him(?) As it turned out, the price was right in the pocket for the tax relief he was seeking.

Wallah! WTF just happened? Talk about synchronicity baby! Lesson learned... Keep all of your options open!

After further discussions with this investor, and since I possessed the proper aviation inspector's license to review this aircraft and its documentation, I arranged to handle the initial aircraft pre-buy performance inspection.

Things became somewhat of a blur immediately thereafter. With Jimmy Buffett's touring opportunity hinging on my delivery of a contract with a capable aircraft and crew, I needed to move fast, and the following days thereafter found me scrambling to secure the inspection on the Fairchild in MSP (Minneapolis), while keeping the Buffett account alive at the same time.

I was young and absolutely rockin' forward at this point! I pulled some bucks together and booked an airline ticket to MSP.

Fairchild F-27 Aircraft - History

https://flyingrocksbook.com/WSj

Upon arrival on a cold and snowy St. Paul (MSP) airport day, I went straight to the aircraft hangar to check on the F-27. As mentioned, it was owned by the Hubbard Broadcasting Company (a local St. Paul TV affiliate station) as the letters HB were placed near its empennage, just behind the rear main door entry.

The empennage is a structure at the rear of an aircraft, also known as the tail or tail assembly.

I mention how the HB initials created another synchronized event in just a bit.

The Fairchild is an interesting critter. Its primary systems operate on pneumatics. Its retractable landing gear, braking systems, nose wheel steering, the main passenger air stair, and propeller brakes, all use compressed air to function. Whereas most large aircraft make use of hydraulic fluids to accomplish these tasks.

Having a pneumatic systems provides for lighter weights, and safety due to lack of flammable hydraulics. And for me, being the technician working on this critter, non-fluids cleanliness was a extra pleasure.

Instead of spoilers (aka, wing brakes) to slow and descend the aircraft down, you'd drop the main landing gear, but not the nose gear, at altitude, as a speed brake in this craft, to lose altitude fast without increasing forward flight speeds.

Even though the Fairchild was originally designed for 32+ passengers in commercial seating configuration, this F-27 was one of very few that was delivered originally with an executive interior arrangement of couches and captain's chairs of 18 seats. Just perfect for the 15 or so individuals that toured with Buffett. Its tail registration number was #20HE. (Two, Zero, Hotel, Echo)

Memorabilia Belt Buckle

Jimmy's chair in front of the F27
Coral Reefers gathered near the back of the aircraft

Since this F-27 was never in airliner configuration use, the flight time on this ship was very low. Low for a large (airline-capable) aircraft. Which meant that it didn't require immediate updates to time-limited serviceable operational parts. A very good thing indeed, because as you can imagine, aircraft can get damn expensive with replacement parts.

Example of a Fairchild F27 Aircraft Taking Off

https://flyingrocksbook.com/d3T

Coral Reefer Band Section - Cheeseburger Airplane...
with Reeferett Deborah McColl

It wasn't the fastest turbo-prop aircraft at 235 knots (270 mph), but it was roomy and reliable. Plenty decent for a touring band that only travels on average less than a few hundred miles between shows. Noting that the stage, light, and sound crew peeps with all of their equipment, couldn't travel by ground more than this in a given day in order to set up before sound check in the next city.

Back in Minnesota, it took me two days to fully inspect the aircraft with all of its components and 2 feet of documented logbooks. It had been maintained impeccably.

It was now time to secure the purchase details with my new investor, and at the very same time continue negotiations with Buffett's management company, which was Front Line Management in Los Angeles, Howard Kaufman and Irving Azoff.

A whole bunch of simultaneous action had to take place within a week, yet it all clicked. It was a whirlwind! The now-secured Buffe5 tour commenced in six weeks. I had started the arrangements to transfer per!nent funds to secure the Fairchild purchase with my aircra" investor, along with the arrangement of a deposit and ini!al contracts with Front Line. Ever tried juggling cats?

Just one more item of importance. Make that a few more considerations... Oh, I needed certified pilots and a flight attendant (or two), aircraft insurance, and repositioning of the airplane to the West Coast. Oh boy, just a few more items to accomplish. Ha!

OK, I was a certified commercial pilot and a flight instructor, yet admittedly not qualified to take over the left captain's seat on this F-27. At least not until I had additional hours under my belt flying this machine in the right throne, the co-pilot's chair. In this instance, at just over 1000 hours of flight time, I needed more, large aircraft experience before allowing myself to even consider flying in the left seat of this bird. However, being a born director, I subsequently learned how to secure sub-contracted flight professionals to handle the captain's position.

Since I had an earlier association with Go Enterprises, which flew large Viscount aircraft (with the same Rolls Royce engines used in the Fairchild), and having met some highly qualified pilots at my local Brackett airport in La Verne So. Cal., it wasn't long before I was able to secure a couple of qualified captains to handle my requirements.

Tour Manager Bobby Liberman Foreground / CRB Background

Now, it was time to gather the airplane crew to finalize pertinent flight check-out rides and ready the ship for Jimmy's first leg of his Cheeseburger In Paradise tour.

For myself to get certified in the right seat as co-pilot and provide flight times for the two recently hired captain associates I sub-contracted, we needed a fair amount of air time flying around in the Fairchild. So, after arranging to have the aircraft ferried from Minneapolis to Los Angeles, we trained by flying to and from as many airports as possible throughout the So Cal area.

I was introduced to a couple of flight attendant trainees along the way, who turned out to be initially worthy of the position. Well, I say initially, because later in this book I describe my wacky episodes with stews and rock bands. I discovered that it's imperative to have a strategic relationship with your clients while maintaining a professional status, meaning, not fraternizing with your paying customers [girls!].

History of Flight Stews / aka: Flight Attendants

https://flyingrocksbook.com/9sQ

During the flight certification process of my hired flight crew, I continued to secure the agreements with Buffett's attorneys, and payment arrangements with his accountants. Including a physical visit to Jimmy's management company.

The Front Line office wanted to visit with me before the tour started. Since I was living in So Cal at that time, it was easy enough to drop by their office. I found myself sitting across the table of Howard Kaufman and Irving Azoff. I didn't realize at that time how powerful these two gentlemen were in the music biz. They were absolute fucking monsters!

Front Line Management was originally owned by Irving Azoff

along with partner Howard Kaufman. Together they managed the careers of (noting just a few back then), Dan Fogelberg, Heart, Boston, Eagles, Aerosmith, Stevie Nicks, along with Jimmy Buffett.

I chatted with Howard and Irving about Jimmy's touring requirements. It's funny now looking back, but I was so busy getting the Fairchild and its crew in readiness for JBs touring, that I hadn't put together a presentation (brochure) package for the aircraft. I only had a few Polaroid snapshots (remember them?) of the (soon-to-be) Cheeseburger airship... LOL!

Anyway, Howard and Irving got Jimmy's road manager, Bobby Liberman, on the speaker phone. They introduced me as their private aircraft pilot and flight consultant for Jimmy's Cheeseburger in Paradise and Son of A Son, tours. Howard (RIP) was the point man and a great guy to communicate with and work for.

Years later I learned that Howard arranged a buy-out with Azoff and subsequently renamed the firm, HK Management. Also later, during my years flying the rock band, Heart, I also worked with one of Howard's partners, Craig Fruin.

Howard Kaufman press release, LA Times

https://flyingrocksbook.com/dZs

Back at the airport where the Cheeseburger plane was parked, I had one more scenario to take care of before departing So. Cal. for the initial Illinois pick-up point of Buffett and the Coral Reefers entourage. I needed to paint over the letters 'HB' on the side of the Cheeseburger's recent plane owner, Hubbard Broadcasting.

While standing on the flight line in Carlsbad Southern California, I was staring at the two-letter initials on the aft side of the Fairchild F-27 airplane of which I was preparing a strategy to paint over them.

Looking at the letters at the entryway of the airplane, a mechanic on his way across the ramp to another project walks behind me shaking a paint can.

Then it hit me! The resolve of the HB was simply to take some paint matching the white background color of the aircraft and edit the letter H to now be a 'J'. Whaala, we now have the letters 'JB' for Jimmy Buffett.

Author/Pilot - HB initials changed to JB

The original Cheeseburger Airplane was now ready for launch. We were set to start Jimmy's first leg of his USA, Son of A Son and Cheeseburger in Paradise tour.

The balance of my flight crew, sub-contracted captains, along with one of the stewardesses, was set to depart within a week to pick up Jimmy and the Coral Reefer Band. Their initial pick-up point was Rockford Illinois on March 4th with the first leg of the tour heading to Davenport Iowa the following day, March 5.

The flight crew and I held a pre-launch party on a Saturday eve the week before the JB launch to celebrate all of the work we had accomplished to this point. We held it at the residence of one of the local flight department's VP, near the Palomar Carlsbad Airport in the San Diego area, where I had the aircraft stationed.

It was rainy and a very windy eve the night of this pre-launch gathering. The next morning early I got a call from the airport facility manager exclaiming that the aircraft had sustained some damage during the storm.

My first impression was, oh shit, what could this be all about?

After arriving at the airport I soon discovered that the damage incurred was at the very front of the aircraft's right side, just aft of the nose cone where the radar was housed.

During that evening, adjacent to the front of the Fairchild, an electric starting cart was positioned, called a GPU (ground power unit) which was used to battery assist with the spool-up of the initial engine start. A jump starter if you will that saves the wear and tear on the ships batteries.

The winds that evening before were so strong that they had forced the GPU's cart off of its wheel blocks and into the direction of the aircraft. It had struck the front of the Cheeseburger plane, just outside and forward to the front landing gear doors. It left a 6-inch gash on the side of the dear gal.

Fuck, that was my first reaction. Yet, after a few moments of allowing a clearer head, I next determined my move to rectify the damage.

My initial repair concern was that if this damage occurred anywhere near the pressurization zone of the nose, such a repair would involve a lot of work. I scrambled under the forward right nose portion of the ship, just inside the front landing gear access point to inspect.

A sigh of relief!

The torn skin damage was limited to the forward, non-pressurized section of the aircraft. I gathered up the parts and went to work on a fairly easy repair that took me the rest of the day.

The fact that I possessed an A&P (Airframe and Powerplant) and IA (Inspector Authorization) certificates, I was capable of providing the appropriate repairs myself, along with the documentation sign-off for the aircraft logbook.

Cheeseburger airplane nose damage location

The to-be soon known as the Cheeseburger Airplane, as subsequently mentioned in the liner notes, along with us pilots of the, You Had To Been There, album, was again ready to launch... Ready for some rock!

A short week passed and we were in the air headed Eastward. The Rockford IL tower announced upon our arrival, "Fairchild Two Zero Hotel Echo (20HE) you're cleared to land," and the ground frequency further instructed us to taxi to the Alpha 1 ramp for parking.

At the very beginning of our flight legs with Buffett, I instructed the crew to wear a certain outfit to start the tour dates... It would be, slacks, a sports coat, and ties. The flight attendant would wear a conservative pantsuit and, a presentable top with a colorful scarf.

Our attire changed radically over time. Within a week on the road, Jimmy suggested we lose the slacks and sports coat and wear the Cheeseburger T-shirts with jeans. We had some fun and interesting airport ramp encounters thereafter. Many corporate pilots flying smaller jets, wearing their flight suites with ties would wander over to our F27 ship, which happened to be one of the largest aircraft on the ramp. They were blown away by our casual attire, some even asked me for a job. LOL!

Our arrival was approximately 2 pm that afternoon in Rockford. I had made arrangements to show the airplane at 4 pm to Jimmy and his personal road manager, Bobby.

It was to be my first meet-up with Buffett. Up to this point all communications had all been through Front Line Management.

A passenger van approached the Cheeseburger aircraft. Private air transportation flyers usually get direct access to the parking tarmac. In this instance, it was a van. Sometimes it would go on to be both, vans and limos. Learned later that vans draw less attention.

As they walked up to the F-27, road manager Bobby said... "Hey look Jimmy, your initials are permanently marked on the side!" Jimmy remarked... "Cool, Michael Lofton, nice touch, I appreciate that!"

Hehe! Little then did they know about the story of the HB/JB initials. Heck, if it weren't for the original HB letters, I probably wouldn't have even thought about putting JB initials on this bird. Thanks, HB for your contribution, and of course, thanks JB for making it even easier to edit to secure your initials on the Cheeseburger Airplane!

I arranged for both Captains I hired to fly and trade off the left seat for the early parts of this tour. I would remain up front in the jump seat as an observer for the initial flight routes. Whereby I would take over the co-captain (first officer right-hand) chair within a few days on the road.

Jimmy Buffett in the jump-seat of the Cheeseburger F-27
I also invited Jimmy to sit in my co-pilot's chair numerous times.

Departure time for the next day's tour launch was set for approximately 2 pm, with the destination Davenport IA., scheduled to land at around 3:30 pm local time. It would be just over an hour's flight. This would allow the band members to go directly to the venue to have a sound check around 4:30 pm and then check into their hotel awaiting departure for the gig later that evening.

The first flight leg of the tour with the Cheeseburger Buffett clan was very smooth and uneventful.

Along with Jimmy, many of the Coral Reefer band members came up to the flight deck to introduce themselves during our first leg of this tour. Even though I had already provided road manager Bobby with a complete schedule of landing facilities, he spent a fair amount of time up front chatting with us about verifying the next several arrival airports and where we'd be parking the aircraft.

Bobby was always on top of scheduling the vans or limos to be awaiting our ramp arrival. Once we parked and shut down our engines, the vehicles would pull right up to the back main airstair of the aircraft.

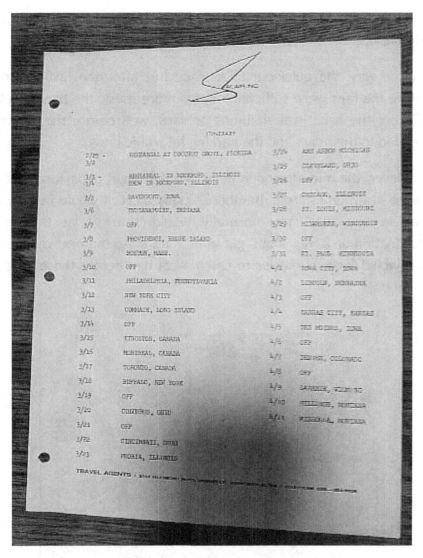

Example of an itinerary

Most rock tours in private aircraft (back then at least) followed this flight scenario... Fly into the airport mid-afternoon. The band would head off to sound check and then they checked into their hotel. The band later that day would head out to gig that eve and afterward return to their hotel until the next day where they'd do it all over again at their next destination.

In some instances, we would do what the music industry called, a 'quick-out'. Once the show was over the band would go directly to the airport, board the craft, and then we would fly them to the next city (gig) location. This arrangement would accommodate for an extended stay at the next stop to allow for more downtime on tour, and some relaxation days off when the itinerary allowed for gig breaks.

By the way, the quick-out took place just after the last encore. While the fans were still chanting for more music the band would slip out the back in their limos or vans, well before the crowds headed to their cars and the parking lot traffic jams.

However, the mid-afternoon fly-in and late-night departures put a slight strain on us crew members to stay alert. It would be a long day in any case. You normally wouldn't arrive at the next destination on a 'quick-out' gig until 2 am or so the next morning. We would force ourselves to catch a cat nap before those longer flight days.

Coral Reefer Band '78 - Some heads are not there (oops)

The hub-and-spoke concept was sometimes used. Whereby, we would arrange to stay in one location, and from there each day we would fly to a destination gig not too far away, and after the gig we would return to the central 'hub' location. The main bummer about this approach was that we never had the opportunity to check out the town of the concert. The flight crew usually stayed at the airport, and we mostly never went to these gigs.

Touring Logistics

Behind the scenes of a major entertainment touring act.

https://flyingrocksbook.com/dD9

By the way, the flight crew would (mostly) make a habit of never staying at the same hotel as the band, as this can and has presented co-mingling problems. You'll discover more about this later. Crew fraternizing... eg., stews especially - argh! When the appropriate time came at gigs, we in the flight crew 'knew' when it was best to retire to our hotel rooms.

Landing at smaller college town airports was a favorite of us flight crew members. The co-captain and I would routinely ask local airport environment folk, like rent-a-car peeps, to come aboard and look around. We always had excess snacks to share.

The temporary wall art was an ongoing band event with displays of individual statements. By the end of the tour, we'd have walls plastered with memorabilia, all long gone unfortunately. Including a photo of Einstein torn from a magazine taped above the toilet and someone scrawled, "Buffett at 80"! As for the gold fixtures in the bath, well, they came with the Cheeseburger bird and were not a requested item from the band. As you can imagine, JB and the CRB were not a pretentious group.

As you can imagine, airplanes require maintenance. The aviation biz provides for 'preventative maintenance' to prevent most all major or eventful episodes. Sometimes certain mechanical events take place. In our instance with JB, we were early on in the Cheeseburger tour whereby the front captain's (left hand) window was showing signs of cracking. But it wasn't cracking. It was de-lamination.

The front windows on aircraft are heated to prevent ice build up which would restrict forward viewing. It's called anti-icing. On the Fairchild, like many aircraft, the two front windscreens had two pains of virtual bullet-proof glass, and sandwiched in between was a thin mylar sheath impregnated with an electrical conductor. De-lamination in this instance was when the mylar started to wrinkle, which made it look like the window was cracking. It needed replacement in any case.

The de-lamination happenend when we were soon to arrive in Boston for an extended stay. On the phone I went to secure a replacement window and rented a couple days in a hangar at Logan airport. Funny enough, right in the middle of a major 1978 snow storm in the North East. Since I was a certified aircraft technician we were able to handle the job. It entailed two days, along with Captain Bill, to secure the new window installation. Bummer, we missed a couple of concerts and it took a big bite out of my profits on that tour. (Mmm, oh well)

Kept that front window as a coffee table for many years. Yet, with all of my life's moves, no telling where it ended up. (mmm)

Fortunately the aircraft did not develop any further mechanical issues for rest of the tour. The Cheeseburger airplane provided the band with a comfortable and safe platform for touring. Of all the aircraft that I had provided Jimmy and the CRB over the years, the Cheeseburger Fairchild remained the front-runner in popularity.

Fingers Taylor
Cheeseburger Airplane '78
Image taken by pilot Michael Lofton

FLASH BACK

Fingers Taylor died shortly after Jimmy's departure. RIP my past life friend (fellow '52 baby boomer). I'm flashing back and remembering the episode with our flight stewardess... A story we will forever keep to ourselves, eh? LOL - Fun Times! Oh, and thanks for making the on-board 'Club Oreo' a real event. It made the airplane a much more fun adventure! I count myself very fortunate to have been a part of our early journey.

Club Oreo was Finger's way of extending his private club to the Cheeseburger airplane. Whereby he blocked off the rear windows of the interior cabin with aluminum foil to darken the environment.

Now might be a good time to mention what gets stocked on the plane in the way of food and drink (other substances aside) to satisfy a group of 15 passengers (on average) per flight. Catering came in many flavors and as an interest in what one would find on a chartered leased aircraft throughout a tour, here are some examples... And brown M&M's weren't usually an issue (hehe - the Van Halen chapter mentions this).

FB thread with the gang @ Jay Surf's Songwriters Joint...
https://flyingrocksbook.com/CHY

For Buffett, (and other bands were similar) the drink stock was... Mount Gay Rum, Vodka, Scotch, Bourbon, beer, and wine, along with non-alcoholic beverages eg., coke, sparkling waters, et. al.

Catered food items included, veggie dip selection, finger (Fingers

Taylor - hehe) sandwiches, fish n' chips, burgers, and other such considerations. However, we found that ordering catering from the local airport presented a scenario whereby it would cost upwards of three times that of having the flight crew grab some take-out from a local deli or such along the way to the airport. Which became a routine check item... including a favorite, pizza, and/or subs. Toss in a few local and national newspapers. Mostly basic requirements.

I remember a flight in the late 70s where Jay Spell, the blind keyboardist, had asked the flight deck crew on the Cheeseburger airplane to sit up front while flying over Niagara Falls. The co-captain and I described to Jay in detail how we viewed the Falls. Jay especially wanted us to use words that had feelings and emotions to describe the landscape below. Very interesting discussion that day.

Blind Jay reading to Finger's - LOL!

Also, in a restroom at a concert, Jay came up to the next urinal and said 'Hi Mike!'... I go, "How the fuck did you know it was me, Jay?"... he goes, "I can tell by the way you're breathing."... I go, "Wow... at least I'm glad you didn't say you could tell by the way I peed!" LOL

The F27 had a Water-Meth injection system on both engines. This allowed us to increase our take-off engine power when needed for a short time during departures. Essentially, it added more density to the combustion chambers to increase the power. It came in very handy on a hot day leaving Aspen Colorado. We had a full boat departure with the JB crew. Along with the WM assistance we further took advantage of an old glider technique by riding a ridge wave out of the valley that day. (hehe)

Most all of our landings were pretty smooth, which subsequently got the band to clap and cheer. Occasionally we'd touch-down a bit stronger, mostly due to higher cross winds, where we'd hear some moans and boos from the passenger cabin... LOL.

Then the time flying over the Northern Rockies into Livingston MT., Jimmy got on the cabin intercom and went, "If you look out your right side you'll see what appears to be snow. It's actually cocaine and what appears to be Aspen trees on the ground are straws. Sorry that you can't be there at the moment. Enjoy your flight!" The cabin peeps cheered and laughed.

The times when JB and the CRB headed down to the Holiday Inn bar and slowly took over the house band and played all together, Werewolves of London, Lawyers Guns and Money, et. al. Or, hiding the stash in the airplane's landing gear well, on the way into Canadian customs. Mmm, I guess "You Had To Be There" to appreciate the moment. (hehe)

Once many months on tour, while we were already rolling down the runway for take-off, we had an indicator light noting that the main rear entry door was ajar. We aborted the take-off and taxied back to parking. While we kept the engines running, I walked back to the cabin and Jimmy asked me what was up. I mentioned the discrepancy and re-locked the main door. Jimmy looked at me and said, "Thank goodness you guys are safety-minded and are on top of situations like this... Thanks!"

Accidents?... Not Ours!

You'll notice that part of this book references entertainment entities involved with aircraft accidents. I have been researching a lot of entertainers who were involved in plane crashes during my decades of flying rock. My primary reason was to investigate why they crashed and what I could learn from such incidences to prevent them from ever happening to my clients. Guess it worked for me, over two decades and applying all of the safety standards learned from those experiences to prevent similar incidences... No crashes! [Thank Goodness!]

Before ever getting into flying bands, I recall the crash of Jim Croce and Otis Redding, and my flashing then upon the idea of how it would be nice to be able to fly rock bands and not crash the airplane [no shit]... Ever since that initial thought and day I had always been interested in the dynamics and subsequent investigations of crashes of famous entertainers.

For example, I had been studying the crash of the popular southern rock band, Lynard Skynard, which had taken place just before our Cheeseburger In Paradise tour with Jimmy. Noting the Nazareth chapter and the initial and closing chapters on Buffett meets Skynard.

On the day of our first departure with Jimmy, I immediately noted the fact that JBs Coral Reefer Band had an ensemble of the same number of band members, including two female backup singers, as the Lynard Skynard band.

At the time it seemed a casual similarity and coincidence, however unbeknown to us at that time, it set the stage for an amazing synchronicity story, later to be experienced on the road.

Jimmy Buffett - Margaritaville (live 1978)

https://flyingrocksbook.com/mUG

Credit Given to YouTuber

Along with the pilots mentioned in the 1978 'You Had To Be There' Album'

So, what's a corporate touring aircraft consultant?

I've been asked, what is a corporate touring aircraft consultant and what does this occupation consist of? I was basically a liaison when I wasn't personally flying the crafts myself, between the chartered or leased aircraft operator and the bands' management. Call it, an over-glorified corporate travel agent. Albeit for big stars.

Here's a general (brief) checklist of items that I used during a band's aircraft touring requirements...

- Verify that the aircraft operator has a valid Federal Regulation part 135 charter or (if applicable) part 125 (actually, part 91D back then) leasing certificate.

- Proof of pilot certifications. Airline Transport Pilot rating (ATP) at least for the Captain position of the aircraft. Along with a minimum amount of flying time in the same type of aircraft being used.

- Verify past five years record clear of any accidents.

- Proof of insurance. Verify required coverage for aircraft and named insured for client and consultant.

- Prepare pertinent flight and consultant contracts and have attorneys from both parties cross-check with any edits.

- Secure payment schedule with approval from both parties' accountants.

- Secure any catering requirements, along with any special items to place on the aircraft.

- Verify pertinent tour itinerary dates regarding departure and arrival times. Secure all Fixed Based Operator (FBO) parking facilities.

- Note any other details with the Road Manager regarding the passenger requirements. Continual communications regarding weather conditions and itinerary updates.

The Federal Aviation Administration (FAA) does a good job of regulating the technical requirements of licensed operators and air travel remains the safest way to travel. However, the complexity of the business required real expertise to find the best operator for a specific itinerary or tour.

One specific occasion the FBO called, while the captain and I were on the way to the airport. They mentioned that the Federal Aviation Administration personnel were there to do a ramp check.

They looked over our paperwork, including aircraft documentation and a verification of our flight licenses. I actually had one of the FAA dudes asking how they might come to work for us. LOL.

The music aviation biz usually followed a protocol whereby when the road manager changed out with another person, the flight consultations also changed. I remained with Buffett from 1978 till 1991 when road manager, Bobby Liberman, then moved on.

Speaking of road management, I captured an interview with Bobby, to discuss some of his experiences...

Bobby Liberman Interview - Jimmy Buffett's Road Manager

FlyingRocksBook.com

https://flyingrocksbook.com/pHX
(Audio Interviews Tab at the FRB Blog)

Also, be sure to check out Bob Liberman's Book about his over a decade of experiences as Jimmy's personal road manager. You'll discover some interesting stories.

My earliest of backstage passes...

Author's Backstage Passes
What a difference one year can make on tour!

The making of Cheeseburger In Paradise

https://flyingrocksbook.com/auC

Grateful Dead Tours
Long Strange Lovely Trips

What A Trip It Was...

Memorabilia

I'm so thankful that the Grateful Dead was an entertainment group that I took care of as a private aircraft consultant for almost 20 years! Luckily, I handled all of their private aircraft touring for the band and crew members whenever they hit the road, mostly in the US and Canada. Right up to the last day, I arranged for the private jet flights ('95) for Jerry from his home base in Northern Cal to Betty Ford's Clinic in Southern California.

Many Dead Heads know that Jerry Garcia was a vital part of the original foundation of the band, as such and after his departure, the Grateful Dead 'avatar' took on another embodiment altogether. I certainly feel (indeed I mean, 'feel') very fortunate to have been a part of this powerful realm of music and aviation history, and, will always cherish my association and memories with this organization!

Probably the best at their craft of providing spin and space jams with their commitment to 'true psychedelic' style, preferring the moment to the artifact, which sets them apart.

Almost 20 years flying (arranging private aircraft tours) till '95 (Jerry's death)... I continue to appreciate and wear it with appreciation and radical gratitude! - Indeed!

The Dead usually used two planes. One for the band, and the other for the crew (when the crew wasn't using buses). The aircraft for the band were usually the size of the corporate Gulfstream II, III, IV, etc. They averaged 14 passenger seats in an executive layout. The crew used smaller ships, like a King Air or a small Lear Jet type, holding 5 or 6. This arrangement allowed the band to travel at the times they found best, and the crew used their aircraft to best fit their production schedules.

I certainly have many backstage production stories to tell. I'm also hoping that you'll join in and contribute to the Flying Rocks Blog and/or Facebook page, with a story you might have regarding your personal experiences with the Grateful Dead (and other bands).

Back in the day, from 1978 – 1995, private aircraft was the way the Dead toured, as many popular bands do to this very day. And no, they didn't take VW buses around the country to get to their gigs.

No, the Dead did not travel by VW vans - LOL!

Their private planes became an efficient tool, which was used for their ability to provide safety and convenience along with their touring schedules and security requirements.

Whenever The Dead hit the road (in the US and Canada) I handled all of their private air transportation touring needs, right up to the very last day of Jerry's departure from our planet. I considered the original GD band as having Garcia at the helm. So, (imho) I outlived the dead (sort of speak, mmm).

The aircraft was a Falcon 10-type jet, the very last private jet flight for Jerry to Betty Ford's place in 1995. It appeared (to me at least) that the clinic might have taken him off the stuff a little too hard, since within a week of his arrival at the treatment facility he endured an early departure from this sphere (dammit!).

Along with the Grateful Dead, I also arranged all the flights for Jerry's Acoustic band along with gig mate, David Grisman. They flew in smaller aircraft, mostly turbo-props like Beechcraft King Airs, and small jet types like Lear-Jets. Also arrange a few flights for Bobby and his Weir/Wasserman (RatDog) gigs.

Beechcraft King Air

https://flyingrocksbook.com/BVH

(Mostly used the Beechcraft aircraft for Garcia Band)

In the earlier days, most of the aircraft that I arranged and consulted for touring the Dead included... King Airs, Lear Jets, Falcon Jets, Gulfstream I, II, and III aircraft, along with the occasional Boeing executive ships.

Example of a Gulfstream

https://flyingrocksbook.com/15z

Most of the subcontracted touring aircraft for my entertainment clients were usually owned by major corporations, like automobile manufacturers to banking institutions. I know, seems like an oxymoron, considering the general anti-establishment of the band to essentially use corporate aircraft to get to all of their gigs, but let's examine why these types of aircraft are essential in daily touring.

As mentioned, it was kind of interesting since many folks approached me with the mention, "I thought the Dead traveled by touring bus or some other ground vehicle, like VW Vans," LOL!

Grateful Dead actually flew in the comfort and style not necessarily known to the average Dead Head. But, by no means were the GD cats pretentious, flying around in corporate style. "Heck No".

Private air travel provided less wear and tear on the group, allowing for more supplementary activities on tour. Such as, extra radio spots and promotional appearances.

The band members were definitely a bunch of cool and wonderful group of folks to work with, inclusive of the very important production team, eg., Manager, Tour/Road Manager, Production Crew Manager, Attorney, Accountant, and the GD Office Staff. Everyone displayed the epitome of professionalism with tremendous support and fun to work with!

Spent many phone calls with Grateful's attorney, Hal Kant. It was fun to work through flight contracts with Hal. He owned a Beechcraft Duke airplane for his personal use. I loved and appreciated the aviation talks with his pilot.

The aircraft contract transactions always required the most expert communication and coordination between legal, accounting, and management. adhering to tight itinerary schedules.

Just like all touring endeavors, the Grateful Dead required strict safety controls over many aspects of their flights. Weather updates, proper airports to handle the aircraft, and timing of gig departures and arrivals throughout their tour itineraries. These were just a couple of my many primary duties as their private aircraft touring consultant.

Here's an image of a typical interior of an average larger jet that they flew on, in those days. This happened to have been somewhere around 1987. A touch on the corporate glitz side. This pic was also used as a publishing support image for my biz back then. A Gulfstream twin-engine jet with an average corporate seating arrangement of 14 passengers.

One of their Gulfstream Interiors

Typically, and like most all of the other bands I handled their private flights, we'd only arrange to carry the basics of road/hotel luggage, bicycles, baby strollers, golf clubs, etc. All of the heavier stage gear ended up in their road (semi) trucks.

Again, I certainly feel very fortunate to have been a part of this powerful realm of music and aviation history, and, will always cherish my association and memories with this organization! I certainly have many stories to tell but, probably not going to divulge every one. I'm sure you'd hold back a few yourself (hehe!). I provide you with some of these stories later in this book.

Regarding one of the greatest rock/jam bands ever... What a long strange trip it was!

Then the call came...

So, one morning I received a call from an associate, apologizing for my loss. "Loss, what loss?" was my response. He then proceeded to update me on Jerry's passing. It was an immediate shock to my system. Saying to myself that this couldn't be true. He was just in rehab at Betty Ford's Place. WTF?!

After the shock had worn off a bit, I took the rest of the day off and headed to town for lunch and a bottle of wine. Upon my arrival at a local favorite restaurant, I was immediately notified by the wait staff that the kitchen was closed. Huh? They said, "Didn't you hear, Jerry Garcia died". OMG, no shit. I said to myself, boy have I've got a story for you. Anyway, I headed out to another establishment to grab a bite and my wine to ponder reflections on the years dedicated to getting GD to their gigs. I guess I've outlived the (the original) Dead.

One backstage engagement with Jerry Garcia had us spending a bit of time talking together. I mentioned how I appreciated my time providing and securing the Dead's air transportation over our many years. Jerry peered over his glasses that had drifted down his nose and looking directly into my eyes and said, "Michael, I want you to know something... I look at your flight service the same way our peeps look at us on stage. You're on my stage performing as your flights that take us safely to our next destination. Don't you ever forget that!" I continue to remember our conversation to this day, like it was yesterday!

Upon Jerry's departure, I wrote a short poem that I presented to the GD Office Staff.

Here it is...

Wing It On An Air Prayer
... For Jerry Garcia
by: Michael J. Lofton

Goodness above, take us upon Your wings and provide for all a smooth flight.
Help steer us from turbulent and unstable endeavors.
May all the passengers on this flight enjoy the same comfortable surroundings.
We thank You for the magnificent views of the billowing clouds, the vast plains, and the towering mountains.
Please let our future resolves to go aloft be assured, and that we may be provided with a safe descent to a soft and secure landing.
And, oh yes, our Guiding Goodness, if You have the seats available, would You consider bringing the attorneys, stock brokers, and Bankers along?
AMEN

Ricky 'Rick' Nelson

The phone call that might have saved his life

Right up front... No, I did not fly Ricky Nelson. I did not arrange for his final flight, however...

Early in December 1985, I was hanging out in my funky converted home attic office in Big Bear City CA, when I received a phone call from Rick Nelson's road manager... He wants a quote on an aircraft for an upcoming winter tour for Ricky (he went with Rick at that time) and his Stone Country Band.

We struck up a short conversation. I asked where he heard about me and he mentioned that he knew of my many years as a flight touring consultant for Jimmy Buffett and The Grateful Dead. He further got a couple of referrals from industry attorneys that I had worked with in the recent past regarding other bands that I had arranged for private touring flights.

Nelson's road manager was looking for a quote on a large twin-piston aircraft... He mentioned that he was seeking a Douglas DC-3. I later learned that Rick's organization owned a DC-3, yet, he was looking for a backup aircraft since theirs was going through an inspection and some repairs, and the ship might not be available to handle their tour.

Ricky Nelson

https://flyingrocksbook.com/3VG

By that point in my aviation consultation career, it was many years that I had stopped quoting tours in older, heavier 'piston' aircraft for entertainment tours. I mentioned this policy of mine to Rick's road manager and he didn't seem to take it very well.

I mentioned that I would be happy to quote him a tour in a newer, quality 'turbine' (turbo-prop) type aircraft. It would cost him a bit more for his tour but I assured him that the safety margins were well worth the extra expense. He continued to push me for a DC-3 tour quote.

I further mentioned as an example why using a twin-turbine provides a safer and better single-engine climb rate compared to heavy twin-piston types, just in case you lose an engine. He seemed rather bored with my attempt to sway his decision.

History of the Douglas DC-3

https://flyingrocksbook.com/1YB

Now, don't misunderstand me about the DC-3... I certainly believe it was one of the coolest and most capable aircraft of its kind for that time period. One of the best! But now It was 1985 and I was on the phone with a road manager for a famous and popular rock singer, one from a popular TV show I watched and liked, who requested an early 1940s vintage aircraft for their tour where newer and safer aircraft were readily available.

FLASHBACK Loved watching the Ozzie and Harriett show in the late 50s... especially when Ricky sang at the end of some episodes. My favorite song of his was, Fools Rush In.
I still watch their Christmas reruns!...

Fools Rush In song

https://flyingrocksbook.com/Xoy

My refusal to book a 40 going on a 50-year-old twin-piston aircraft for Rick's tour remained steadfast.

The conversation with Rick's road manager remained somewhat short since he was adamant about retaining the Douglas DC-3 ship for this gig. I did my best to let him know that I could come close to his requested bid price in a safer and more efficient bird, but he didn't want to discuss paying a dime more for his air transportation cost.

We finished up our phone conversation and I didn't think much more of it. Since I had quoted many tours at this point in my career with my aviation projects, winning and losing contracts along the way was just par for the average business year. I figured that all I could do was provide the information and pertinent available aircraft and then it was up to this road management and their legal team to decide if he or they were to proceed with me or not.

As it turned out, they decided that they were able to handle the tour after all with their existing Douglas craft.

Then the next phone call came regarding Nelson.

On New Year's Eve, just over a month after my conversation with Nelson's road manager, I received a call from my neighbor penny-ante poker buddy friend, Bob... he goes, "What do you think about the accident tonight?"... he continued, "I mean, you talked with the road manager awhile back, right? You must have an opinion about the crash?"

"What crash?" was my response.

I was working late into that night and didn't have the TV on for news feeds in my small attic office, nor any other sourcing for immediate news (mmm, pre-Internet).

My initial thought was this buddy of mine must be pranking me (he had done such in the past) and since it also being New Year's Eve and all, it seemed only fitting he'd be messin' with me.

These were times when you couldn't just pull up social media for instant reference to events. I popped the TV on to a news outlet and sure enough, there was that mention of an accident concerning Rick and his band.

Once it soaked in, my worst thoughts gathered in remorse for maybe not pushing harder in talking Rick's road manager out of the DC-3 aircraft and into a different ship. Fate was raising its head. I couldn't sleep the rest of that night! But in retrospect, I did my best to move him into a turbine.

Then, only days after the funeral, initial bullshit rumors and newspaper reports suggested cocaine freebasing was one of several possible causes for an in-flight fire and the plane crash... which didn't sit just right with me. So, I decided to follow up with some further research.

The crashes of entertainers always had my invested interest. Researching and learning the reasons 'why' such crashes occurred, allowed me to include prevention protocols in my touring flight services to avoid the same from ever happening with my clients.

A few months hence this unfortunate event, I was chatting with a music attorney associate of mine. The Nelson crash came up in our discussion. He mentioned that he knew one of the lawyer's in the case for the Nelson family and that if I wanted he'd arrange a meeting with him to discuss what he had gathered to that point regarding his investigation.

"Heck Yeah!" was my response. Shortly thereafter I was able to secure that meet-up with the attorney.

I flew a small aircraft for which I had to my avail from Big Bear

City Airport to Fullerton Airport in California for the subsequent follow-up luncheon with the Nelson family attorney, which took place inside the Fullerton airport cafe. I was very interested in the attorney's take on what he could reveal to this point on any post-crash updates.

Since the attorney was still going through the trial process, at that time he was very limited in his ability to disclose much of what he knew.

He did mention one specific point to me. Knowing that part of my aviation background was the holder of an aircraft Inspection Authorization certificate along with an Airframe and Powerplant technician license, he leaned over the cafe table and in a lowered tone said, "Michael, a possible loose 'b-nut, that's all I can say right now." Of course, this info remained to myself.

Well, as it turned out and according to the NTSB (National Transportation Safety Board), it was discovered that the aircraft's supplemental main cabin heater was suspect. A loose 'b-nut' where the fuel line attached to the heater could have created some leakage of fuel which possibly ignited the fire.

Mmm, it appears I had some inside info before the public ever had it available.

As a certified aircraft technician (A&P and IA) I had many experiences dealing with persnickety self-functioning (and non-functioning) gas cabin heaters. I can surely tell you that those critters were for sure notorious for in-flight malfunctions. So, this inside info didn't come as a major surprise.

The DC-3 is a non-pressurized aircraft and needs to remain under a certain altitude (generally below 12 thousand feet) without the use of supplemental oxygen requirements... In any case, it gets damn cold at these higher flight altitude levels. A cabin heating system was required to keep the temps comfortable in the cabin.

I was later able to retain the post-crash National Transportation Safety Board (NTSB) investigation report to reference all of the crash details. It's 4 inches thick!

NTSB file (4 inches thick!)

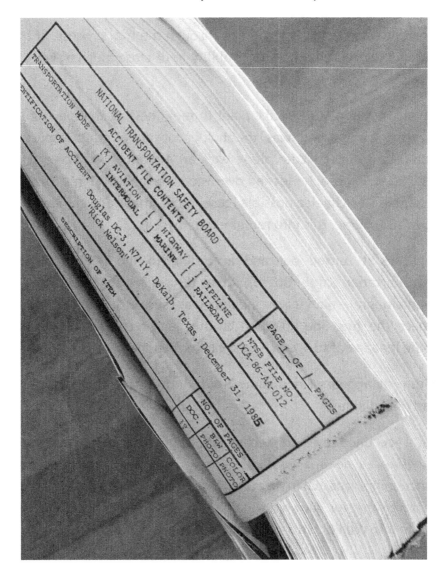

The early NTSB findings and subsequent follow-up research data noted indeed that the aircraft heater was the source of the in-flight fire, within the cabin area where Rick and the band were seated, with a ton of smoke to go along with the flames. This sucked!

Now, I'm not going to do a deep dive into all the stuff that had been documented during this horrible episode, since many books and online dissertations cover these events in complete detail. You'll find a couple of those references in my citations noted below. I will note, however, that every time I flew a band or entertainer, these simple reminders secured my focus on flight safety during every one of my flight consultations.

To quote a couple the Wiki citation references... Band members shared fears with their families about the DC-3's airworthiness. Lead guitarist Bobby Neal's wife Phyllis, urged him not to board the airplane. Bassist Patrick Woodward told his wife Jodie about the two emergency landings. *"He said he was going to die in that airplane and he said it seriously"*, she recalled.

Lori Russell, wife of sound technician Clark said, *"I hated the plane because every time he went on it I thought it would be the last time. The band hated the plane"*.

Laurie Barzie, the sister-in-law of pianist Andy Chapin, added, *"He didn't want to go on that airplane"*. Barzie said Chapin told her *"that it was a really bad plane. he didn't trust it. He always talked to my husband about it, that he didn't trust the airplane, that all the guys felt the same in the band"*.

     NTSB is the National Transportation Safety Board. They are called in on investigations involving deaths as they relate to post-aircraft crash scenes. The FAA, Federal Aviation Administration, handles almost all other smaller airplane instances that do not involve fatalities.

According to the National Air Transportation Board (NTSB) N711Y was registered to Century Equipment, Inc., Los Angeles, California. The airplane was sold to Rick Nelson on the 2nd of May 1985 but was never re-registered. BTW, not being a registered aircraft did not relieve the Nelsons from ownership operational responsibilities.

I want to mention a few words about the DC-3, otherwise known as the Gooney Bird. To quote the Smithsonian History of Flight -

"Until the advent of the incomparable Gooney Bird, long-distance flying was a chancy and uncomfortable proposition."

In 1943 the DC-3 not only gave the Allies a reliable troop and material transport but allowed Bob Hope's Troupe, Glen Miller's Band, and other entertainers of that era to entertain troops on the far flung battlefields.

The ubiquitous Gooney went on to fly the "Hump" over the Himalayas into China. The civilian versions went on to serve as dependable cargo carriers. Roomy and reliable, the Gooney Bird was yesterday"s flying tour machine.

Further details about this DC-3 crash...

Here:
https://flyingrocksbook.com/gMh

And Here:
https://flyingrocksbook.com/fBJ

Besides these URL locations, also refer to these books to expand your knowledge on the Rick Nelson aircraft crash.
- Falling Stars by Rich Everitt, page 102
- Music's Broken Wings by William P. Heitman, page 353

Barry Manilow

One of many Tour books provided to crew personnel

5 years flying Barry. I don't have a long story, since almost all of our flights went fairly flawlessly. However, there's always a story or two to be told. All of my flight consults were securing the plane and the flight crews on his touring ventures. I was not his personal pilot, just his over-glorified travel agent, or in my instance (aka) a private aviation flight touring consultant.

Most of the flights during my Manilow half decade that I had arranged and managed were placed in a Gulfstream 1 aircraft. This was the (popular touring) semi-stand-up cabin, twin turboprop. It had Rolls Royce Dart turbine engines with Dowty Rotol propellers, driving the machine's propulsion. In executive layout seating arrangement, it would accommodate 12 passengers comfortably. It was also used in the airline industry serving approx 24+ passengers.

Gulfstream 1 - TurboProp

https://flyingrocksbook.com/FH1

Lots of bands were placed in the Gulfsteam Aircraft

https://flyingrocksbook.com/fnp
Credit given to YouTuber

Gulfstream interiors are rather cozy

btw... The earliest of aircraft propellers were named, Airscrews. Here is the history of the propeller (airscrew) used on the Gulfstream 1. The same props were also installed on the Fairchild F27 Cheeseburger airplane and the Viscount, extensively used for my entertainment consultations.

Dowty Rotol Propellers (Airscrews)

https://flyingrocksbook.com/ROM

I used the Gulfstream 1 on a ton of client contracts. It fit the profile of many entertainers perfectly at that time. The thing was, however, when a band needed more that 12 seats, they were nudged into the next level at that time, eg., Fairchild, Viscount, Convair, etc., which meant more bucks for sure.

At one point during my years with Barry as his flight touring consultant, I got a call from Victor, the road manager. He goes, "Michael, did you know that we haven't had air-conditioning in the airplane for a few days now?" I go, "No Way!".

It was during some hot summer touring legs when the aircraft is on the ramp, or within a few thousand feet in the air, you need air conditioning to stay cool. Once you reach higher altitudes the AC is not required so much as the outside air temp drops pretty fast. On average, it's about 3.5 degrees Fahrenheit drop for every 1000 feet of elevation you gain.

After that phone chat with Victor, I immediately got on the horn and chased down the owner and operator of the airplane who I had secured the flight contract with for this particular tour. He happened to also be the captain of the bird.

I go to the captain, "I just got word that the air-conditioning on the ship is inop, is that right?" He goes, "Michael, I'm trying to secure a fix but it might take me a while."

Now, I can dig the fact that some time is required to fix a discrepancy, but this captain has gone on almost a week to attempt the fix, and for that matter, he never alerted me to the problem. I learned via the road manager, which is not good. The contract that I had arranged with him called for pertinent maintenance items to be secured and fixed within 5 days.

But that wasn't the only rub. Apparently, via the grapevine, this contracted operator was running low on cash and was in arrears on his past fueling bills on the airplane. Oh crap, not good.

I alerted the captain that in the meantime I would arrange to have an air-conditioning ground unit available at the next couple of airports before departure to keep the cabin cool for Barry and his entourage upon departure, yet, he would need to have the air-conditioning repaired within 5 more days. Essentially cutting him slack on another week+ of travel.

After a few days, I called the captain to check in. No response. I must have called twelve times over 24 hours. No response. Now I'm getting a bit miffed!

Finally, Victor calls and claims that the pilot/owner/captain has suggested that he can't fix the air-conditioning due to a scheduling conflict. I'm thinking to myself, wtf, a scheduling conflict? I'm now learning that it might be more than that. It could be because of a monetary conflict, or a lack of funds on his behalf to arrange and fix.

Crap!

So now I'm thinking to myself, what are my options? I could continue to try to babysit both sides of the equation, the Gulfstream owner and the road manager. Since the aircraft contract has been broken there doesn't seem to be any direction on the aircraft owner's side to remedy.

It might be time to move to the next stage and secure another Gulfstream (or very similar) aircraft. I started working on the latter. Oh, the fun (at times) of being in the aircraft charter consultation industry.

My phone dialing started in the hunt for another ship to handle the balance of this particular Manilow tour. I checked the payment schedule for the aircraft operator, which was usually segmented into numerous payouts during most tours. It happened that their next payment was due in a few days.

I finally got on the phone with the captain. He definitely seemed a bit frantic. Not good in my aviation pilot book. He told me that he needed another few weeks, but wasn't even sure that the air-conditioning would be fixed by then. Mmm, beyond knowing that he was gently defaulting on his aircraft contract, I further knew that the AC being inoperative wasn't the only discrepancy, I needed to make him aware that I was searching for another operator to take over the rest of the tour.

This is where business conflicts suck!

Off I went, knowing that I needed to secure another qualified aircraft (with a working AC no less!) to take over the rest of the tour. I found that aircraft. I started the procedures to dispatch the replacement craft. All the usual consultation stuff. Aircraft certificated papers, insurance, pilot qualifications, and contracts, inclusive of money transactions. (OMG).

Communicating this to the existing Gulfstream operator caused a bit of a riff. He was animate about keeping the tour under his belt, yet knowing that he couldn't deliver with the AC fix and past fuel bills. Perhaps even stumbling on other uncovered scenarios.

I was in communication with the road manager, Victor. I told him of my plan to secure another ship for their tour. He was totally on board and understood my dilemma and concern about the situation.

In the meantime, the Bronx / Brooklyn card emerged.

Victor calls. "Hey, Michael I know we are supposed to pick up the new chartered aircraft in a couple of days from now, but get this... The pilot/owner of the existing touring craft just slipped a note under Barry's hotel room door. It reads (paraphrasing), "Barry, can you cut a Bronx neighbor a break, as a Brooklyn boy?"

OMG, WTF, really?

I'm somewhat dumbfounded. OK, I've now substantiated the replacement Gulfstream, but what am I to do with a note like that?

I guess the captain of his soon-to-be-replaced Gulfstream thought that since Barry was born near him, he'd get a break. Oh man, the stuff that happens on the road. Anyway, thank goodness that Victor covered my ass during this transition to the next Gulfstream. Again sometimes business dealings have consequences whereby one side or the other gets their (airplane) feathers ruffled, or in this instance, sent home with their tail between their legs.

Business was business in this case, and if the aircraft contract could not be fulfilled, then steps had to be taken to clear the matter up. Unfortunately, this required a complete change-out of aircraft to handle the discrepancies at hand.

I met Barry only once briefly backstage in Denver CO late in our flight ventures. His last tour was winding down and I was there on this last leg, whereby I had arranged a Lear Jet-35 standing by at the local airport awaiting his private flight back to Los Angeles. The entertainment touring industry was slowing down at this point, and after 5 years of working with his staff, Barry's touring schedule was coming to a close, at least for a while.

Barry kindly shook my hand as we chatted for a few moments. He goes, "Hey Michael, it's been 5 years of us working together and this being the first time we've personally met... That's crazy, eh? I want to thank you from the bottom of my heart for all of your background work and the way you have handled all of my touring flights! You've been the best in making them all come off smoothly!" My response was simply, "Thanks Barry, I've enjoyed the ride, for sure!"

Lightening, Smoke, and the Border Crossings

- Nazareth's Roadies -

After popping through the other side of a severe squall line of thunderstorms, heading the opposite direction of our route just west of Chicago, the Boeing 727 United Airlines captain came on the horn and asked, "What kind of aircraft are you?" I responded as the co-pilot in the right seat of our ship, "We're a Vickers Viscount (vī-ˌcourìt)." With a slight chuckle in his deep voice the United captain responded, "If I were you I'd turn around right now and find a suitable airport to wait for this weather system out." Damn, not what we wanted to hear!

This Nazareth flight started with a pickup in Phoenix, Az. (PHX) On July 1, 1979. July... It was hot, even though our departure time was close to midnight. About 97 degrees that evening. Essentially, the Density Altitude was up there. However, we did have ample runway length to handle our full-load departure.

Density Altitude

https://flyingrocksbook.com/g4p

Along with my hired experienced Captain (I flew as first officer on this trip) we stood ready on the ramp of Phoenix International Airport for the ground arrival of Nazareth's crew.

This was one of those rare occasions where we'd fly the road/stage crew (aka roadies) only, without band members aboard. It's rare but every bit as interesting and enjoyable as flying bands and VIPs!

I had secured a very short-term lease for a Viscount 700 series aircraft from a corporation in Denver for this venture. It had a modified interior of 8 club seats up front just forward of a solid wall (bulkhead), with open space for cargo thereafter. The aviation biz calls these types of aircraft 'combi-configured' ships.

Nazareth - Hair of the Dog

https://flyingrocksbook.com/LMP
Credit given to YouTuber

Nazareth's Viscount

This short week of flying would have us crisscrossing North America from Phoenix (PHX) to Toronto (CYYZ) and back to Oakland, CA, (OAK) as Nazareth was ending their World Music Festival tour.

Airport ID codes

https://flyingrocksbook.com/Pbo

The lease on the Viscount was June, 30 thru July 4, 1979, to handle this Nazareth itinerary. The aircraft agreements were negotiated with Nazareth's management under the Federal Aviation Regulation (FAR).

If you're interested, we flew under what was then called, Part-91 Subparts D & F, of FAR operations. It later became known as Subpart K and FAR 125. Not to be confused with FAR part 135 for charter aircraft. I know, a mouthful for sure.

Nazareth's management had signed the appropriate aircraft and flight crew contracts, just days before departure and subsequently transferred the required deposit money to secure the start of this trip, with the balance of funds to be paid before the last leg.

Arrangements were secured to fly myself and the captain to Denver to pick up the aircraft and handle the preflight criterion.

With the hired captain in the left seat and myself in the right, we repositioned the aircraft (aka: ferried, moving an airplane from one location to another without passengers) from Denver International Airport to Phoenix International to prepare for the first Nazareth leg.

Shortly after 10 PM the cargo and crew members arrived at Phoenix International Airport, PHX.

The Nazareth crew were a nice bunch of fellows. They had that road-crew road-wear look to them. They had been on the road for a fair amount of time before we met them on the Phoenix airport ramp.

No doubt these last legs of their tour would be long. The crew guys mentioned how they looked forward to finally getting back to their homes with family and friends within a few days.

It took us a good couple of hours to load their complete stage gear, inclusive of all instruments, monitor equipment, back-line, and some forward throw (aka: front-of-house sound speakers and mixing boards, etc). All required a lot of cargo netting and tie-down straps!

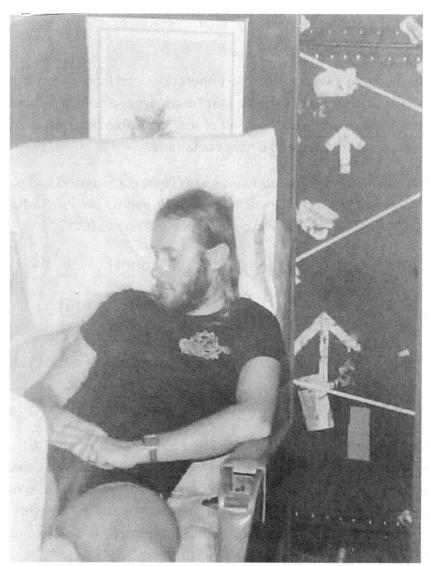

One of Nazareth's crew in the first-class club seating section (gear strapped-down behind the bulkhead)

The Nazareth band members themselves would not be riding with us on these flight legs. They'd take first-class airliner seats for these longer-distance flights. It would be 7 roadie passengers (PAX in aviation terms) that put the live show components together for each gig. A ball-busting adventure for the unsung heroes of the live entertainment touring industry.

Before leasing the aircraft to Nazareth I determined through a lot of conversation with their management the amount of cargo in cubic feet needed to secure their transportation needs. These chats, my own deep research, along with the flight time requirements, influenced my final decision as to the type of aircraft to handle this tour.

I needed to arrange with airport operations and loading conveyor belt ramp personnel (the type that feeds luggage onto the plane). Once loaded, we already had all of the applicable tie-down straps to secure each stage equipment containers.

Around midnight-thirty on July 1st with flight plan in hand and pax and cargo loaded, our Phoenix departure had us planning a fuel stop in Salani (SLN) KS. with continuance to Toronto (CYYZ)

Vickers Viscount (vī-ˌcouṅt)

https://flyingrocksbook.com/CsS

Our Viscount 700 series was one large lumbering aircraft. Each of its four Rolls Dart Royce Tubo-Prop engines had a shaft horsepower of about 1500 (shp) and lifted an average gross weight of approximately 60 thousand pounds (30 tons!) with a forward drive cruise speed of approximately 260 knots (around 300 miles per hour).

The aircraft wasn't that fast with its average cruise airspeed. It was however a very popular ship at the time and sure worked great as a comfortable ride for the touring industry for many years. Hauling a good amount of entertainers, and in our instance, an additional cubit feet of mostly freight.

The only problem was that the Viscount was built and meant for shorter flight lengths. Yet, it was the only aircraft able to handle our job of hauling gear and pax back and forth across North America, even if it required stops for fuel.

Explanation and History of knots = miles per hr
Note: Kts = mph eg., 1 kt = 1.15078 mph

https://flyingrocksbook.com/zNb

It was indeed a hot motha' on the ramp that evening in PHX. The ramp temperature reflecting off the airport asphalt tarmac was hovering at or above 110+ Fahrenheit degrees, at midnight no less! Which (again) meant we were dealing with a density altitude way up there.

Since our ship was at maximum take-off weight with full fuel, cargo, and passengers (pax), we needed to determine the best runway for departure... We knew it would take every bit of runway PHX could offer for our lumbering beast to become airborne.

We requested the longest runway for lift off and the tower suggested runway 26 with a length of approximately 11,500 feet. The number 26 indicates runway direction on a compass... eg., 260 degrees heading.

It took every bit of 10,000 feet to get the Viscount beast off safely that evening!

These were the flights that had you make extra sure all engines were operating in the green to their max horsepower delivery with a little praying that one didn't let you down on takeoff... hehe.

Our fuel stop in SLN (Salina, KS) would be about 4 and a half hours, hence our midnight PHX departure. With the loss of a couple of hours allowing for time zone adjustment, our landing into SLN local time was approximately 7 am.

We had our required flight crew rest the day before this venture, but eastward flights with the sun coming up still had us yawning in those early sunrise hours. Yep, we had hot coffee on board.

Our fuel was topped off within 45 minutes on the ground in SLN. It would take another 4 hours of flight from our Salina fuel stop to arrive in Toronto. We would lose another hour to the crossing of the next time zone.

After flying all night and day, albeit most of it in modified sleep positions in upright airline seats, the roadies had a crazy and hectic day and night still ahead of them setting up the stage gig gear once again.

What a job! Would you really want to be a roadie? However, they sure are some of the most good-natured folk on tour. And talk about experiences.

As the saying goes in the music industry, "Bands make it rock... Roadies make it roll!"

The Road Crew

https://flyingrocksbook.com/SmC

The road crew (or roadies) are the technicians or support personnel who travel with a band on tour, usually in sleeper buses, and handle every part of the concert productions except actually performing the music with the musicians. This catch-all term covers many people: tour managers, road managers, production managers, stage managers, front-of-house and monitor engineers, lighting directors, lighting designers, lighting techs, guitar techs, bass techs, drum techs, keyboard techs, pyrotechnicians, security/bodyguards, truck drivers, merchandise crew, and caterers, among others.

Our schedule required us to be in Toronto in time to allow for more than an hour to unload the gear (it took less time to unload than load.) Nazareth's roadies would also need to transport their gear to the venue (gig) in order to build up their stage and make ready for band sound check by 5pm that same day.

We taxied up to the private airplane parking ramp at Toronto CYYZ Int'l around noon local. Customs cleared us immediately and the unloading of the cargo commenced.

Customs for private aircraft have always been generally easier than commercial flights. Yet, entering the United States was always more of a hassle (as you'll soon discover). Generally, in Canada, they know ahead of time when a touring entertainment act is arriving to play a few shows, making the process of entering their country fairly painless (at least back in those days!).

Immediately after securing the Viscount, my hired captain and I went off to our hotel ... Unfortunately, no time was available to fit in a Nazareth show on this stop. (Bummer!)

It was required of us (the flight crew) to have plenty of rest and sleep in order to start our next, westward bound leg to Oakland, CA. within 36 hours. So off to snooze and rest we went.

Many times as a pilot flying rock stars you're never allowed the time to hang out at the gig. Only when ground time provides for ample rest. Usually it requires a couple of days in one spot.

The opportunity for us flight crew members to hang out back-stage, eat plenty of food, watch the concert, and generally chuck and jive with the band was always a pleasure and experiences I'll remember for life. Including some non-mentionable backstage shenanigans (lol!).

There are many times, however, that even if we couldn't stay for the complete concert due to flight crew rest hours, before the gig we'd normally slip by early enough to catch a free catered meal backstage. Always more food prepared then was ever eaten.

The morning of July 3 around 10am the Nazareth roadies and gear showed up on the Toronto ramp. The first thing the road manager did was open his anvil briefcase and hands me the required funds to secure the final leg of this flight, which included all the crazy expenses like fuel (the Viscount would easily eat close to 300 gallons per flight hour), along with crew per deim, parking and loading fees, insurance, etc. Yep, most of the bucks went to aircraft operational expenses. The remaining profit was otherwise claimed on my (damn it!) taxes.

It took a couple of hours (once again) to load all of Nazareth's cargo at the Toronto International ramp.

Nazareth stage cargo tied down behind passenger bulkhead

Securing (tied down) the cargo according to flight regulations (the FAA), especially in combi-configured aircraft, is precise and demanding. Lots of nets and straps and tie-downs! I was quite anal about such matters. The fact that at any given moment the Feds could cruise up and ask to come aboard to inspect and determine your tie-down procedures and paperwork. If it wasn't right you'd risk a canceled flight.

Finally with the band gear loaded and secured along with the 7 Nazareth roadies aboard the craft, off we flew, heading west to Oakland, via a pre-arranged customs and fuel stop in Nebraska, which would be about four and a half hours into our first flight leg.

The arrival in Oakland after our mid-continent fuel and customs stop was set for approximately 7 PM local PST. The crew was expecting to unload and get ready for their July 4th On The Green

Festival gig in Oakland Stadium, hosted by the famous (and controversial) west coast rock promoter, Bill Graham.

Shortly after departure a couple of the fellas came up to the flight deck and chatted with us. We learned that a few of them were also the roadies for the Lynyrd Skynyrd band a couple of years earlier (Oct '77.) They told us the story of how they requested that they remove themselves from their private aircraft and traveled instead via bus, just a couple of flights before the unfortunate LS airplane crash in Gillsburg, Mississippi.

We wanted to know more about why they, the roadies of Skynyrd at the time, felt the need to get off their airplane and go bus.

One road crew member mentioned to us that some of the other roadies had felt uncomfortable riding on the Skynyrd airplane and just had a sense, a hard nudge if you will, to get off and seek ground transportation instead. He described it as, "a mysterious gut feeling strongly telling us what to do!" Oh man, Skynayrd comes up again. Refer to the similar Jimmy Buffett experience chapters...

FLASH BACK *In another part of this book, you'll discover that I had a continual wacky relationship with Lynyrd Skynyrd (and other rock entertainers that had a brush with airplane crashes) and how they [all] related (in a reflective way) to many of my flight experiences. No, I never crashed an airplane, but unlike many episodes no doubt in your life, whereby, synchronicity becomes an everyday part of your life, these brushes with fate were touch points of some interesting 'wow' events.*

Lynard Skynard Crash

https://flyingrocksbook.com/g8v

We knew our westward flight between Toronto Canada and Oakland CA would be a long one, about 11 hours total with our Nebraska fuel stop. However, we certainly didn't anticipate the events along the way that would extend our trip length even further.

After our 1pm local departure from Toronto and being airborne into our flight for a little over a couple of hours, just at the western edge of Illinois, approaching Iowa, our in-flight weather radar started painting numerous and ominous thunder cells ahead... aka, a squall line.

We were flying toward a massive line of thunderstorms!

Weather was predicted to be somewhat tricky along our route, however, it wasn't forecasted to be that nasty... but it was!

As we approached the squall line we noticed that it didn't allow for any openings for passage. Especially in an aircraft that couldn't fly above 28K feet! Unfortunately, Viscouts didn't have the capability of flying much higher.

So, even though our Viscount was well equipped with weather radar and anti-icing, it did have its maximum altitude limits of flying in the upper 20s (in thousands of feet). A flight level closer to 35 thousand feet was required that day to even consider negotiating the weather that lurked ahead of us.

Thunderstorms, let alone squall lines, are nothing to play around with when it comes to airplanes. The up-and-down drafts alone are extreme and severe. The ride, even by giving them a wide-berth, is usually a bitch and it's required, and a damn good idea, to work well around T-storms in every circumstance.

Explanation of a thunderstorm and a squall line

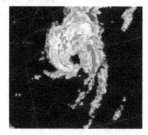

https://flyingrocksbook.com/c37

As we approached the squall line we could see visually and via our radar scans that it didn't look very friendly whatsoever and, furthermore, it didn't show any openings to sneak through.

Again, our Viscount could only reach a certain altitude as its maximum service ceiling was on average 28,000 feet.

The tops of these thunder bumpers (another aviation term) were in excess of 38k, at least 35,000 feet on average. Not something we could even consider tackling by flying over. Through it, however, was only a consideration with plenty of room between Thunder-cells.

The captain from United Airlines, punching through the squall line from the other side coming toward our direction, was communicating with center (air traffic flight following). We were still pondering the decision of whether or not we're going to go in and try to find a hole in the weather system. Lucky for us, that United Airlines captain gave us a flight reporting right in the air, which is the best type of reporting that you can get.

After popping through the other side of a severe squall line of thunderstorms, heading the opposite direction of our route just west of Chicago, the Boeing 727 United Airlines captain came on the horn and asked, "What kind of aircraft are you?" I responded as the co-pilot in the right seat of our ship, "We're a Vickers Viscount." With a slight chuckle in his deep voice the United captain responded, "If I were you I'd turn around right now and find a suitable airport to wait this weather system out."

Damn, not what we wanted to hear! But safety always comes first!

It didn't take us but a few minutes to make the decision right then and there to say, nope, we're not going to attempt to go through it, even if the radar showed an inkling of a pocket to consider flying thru. We're going to turn around and secure the closest suitable airport to land this baby and wait until there are better weather conditions.

The decision to wait the weather system out was one thing, Finding an airport with suitable runway requirements was the easy part. What we needed additionally was to locate an airport that had not only a suitable landing and departure runway, we required customs to be available for private aircraft. At the last moment, no less!

The captain and I both looked at each other and mentioned with slightly dismayed humor, this should be fuckin fun. Errr!

Flying from Canada over the border to the US, we originally had customs set up in Nebraska. As it turned out, we're not only going to need to make a last minute change to locate a private aircraft customs airport near us, we'd need to call en-route now and cancel our original Nebraska customs point of entry.

In aviation, there are those times when a 'lot' to take care of can emerge at any given point. This was one of those times. Our flight deck was very busy. Those were them days when you had to rely on air-to-ground phone communications, since cell phones and the digital age didn't exist.

I alerted the head Roadie and he accepted the fact that going the safe route, even if it delayed their west coast arrival, was very acceptable considering the circumstances.

So now we're looking on our flight charts. Again, nothing was digital back then, so no gps mapping on the flight panel or what you have on your smartie phone today. Determining who had a certified US customs office at an airport big enough to land our Viscount beast of a ship was a chore to say the least.

Chicago Midway Airport.

Midway went from a very popular airport in Chicago in the early years to a very quiet airport with only one operating terminal by the late 70's and the early 80's. I believe it was Midway Airlines flying in and out of it at that time. Today Midway has (I'm pre-assuming) returned to be quite a robust airport.

We had already passed the Chicago area, heading for our intended border crossing entry point in Lincoln, NE. Anyway, it was now time to scratch that itinerary. Time to turn around and head for Midway, Chicago.

The problem arose as we alerted the government border customs folks in Chicago Midway of our required change in flight plans for customs assistance.

Utilizing our air-to-ground flight phone, I called in to make a request to have a customs agent or agents available for our re-routed arrival at Midway.

We could tell by their voices that they weren't too happy at all about our last-minute request. "Sorry guys" was my remark, "but a weather emergency is not our fault. We're heading your way and will be on the ground in about 45 minutes."

Oh boy, this should be real fun [not!], again, was our banter in the cockpit.

As mentioned, the customs dudes weren't too happy with our last minute requests (the Gov could be a hassle if you rocked their little boat), but they had to honor our request because we had been stuck with a weather phenomenon that required deviation. We needed an airport with the ability to accommodate us. Even if it was last minute and a hassle for them.

We made arrangements to come in and park the craft at the U.S. Customs terminal at Midway that handled private aircraft.

At that time I sported some pretty long hair (a bit hippy-looking) and in a T-shirt, along with the Captain, who was also in casual attire. We did have sports jackets, however... haha

As we shut down the last of our four turbines, two guys in suits strolled out toward our Viscount. Once our onboard post-flight checklist was secured we popped open the entry airstair.

As we came down the craft's steps the custom dudes asked if they had permission to come aboard. We obliged them.

With the customs request and as they came up the airstair they turned to their right to see seven scraggly-looking roadie dudes. You know, those hippy-looking guys sitting in the club seating arrangement, with a door just behind them. One of the customs fellas goes, "What's behind the bulkhead door?"

We opened the door up and there was this, uh, forever line of cargo cases, packed ceiling high and going on for probably 50 feet! Well, we knew it was sound gear, but it could have been anything as far as customs were concerned.

The government suits just looked at me and the captain and just shook their heads and remarked... "Oh boy, are you guys kidding us!?"

"You know," remarked one of the customs guys, "we could have you unload all of this stuff right now, just to prove to us that it's really sound gear as you say."

Oh Crap, knowing it took us hours to load this beast of an aircraft, the thought of doing that was insanely unsettling! We still needed to reach the left [west] coast (OAK) now before the cut-off time of 10 PM ... jeez... We just might be fucked!

LOL

However, the two Gov guys didn't immediately require such

removal and inspection of the equipment. They did, however, view our manifest, the complete list of our cargo carriage, pertinent aircraft certification documents, along with our flight licenses.

We then asked customs if we could, while they reviewed the paperwork, go inside the flight service station, which happened to be next door to their customs office, to check weather updates and take care of canceling our original flight plan. They agreed, and off we went.

The captain and I continued to check out the weather. We figured if customs wanted us they'd know where to find us.

After about 30 minutes on the ground, it became evident that the weather system was breaking up, which provided us with a window of opportunity to get back in the air.

We left the flight service station with new weather briefings in hand and headed over to the customs office to see what the suits had in store for us. Their doors were locked. Nobody's there. WTF?

OK, so customs must be on the aircraft along with the roadies.

Nope, nobody there, including the roadies! Uh, really? now WTF!?

It appeared that our passengers had taken off somewhere. We had no idea where. All the buildings close by were either the flight service station, where we just got our weather details, or the customs office, which was locked up!

"Isn't this just dandy," I remarked to my Captain.

We looked around and noticed a couple hundred yards away was the one and only operating airline terminal, adjacent to our private parking ramp. It appeared to be the only place our roadies could have walked to, maybe visiting the restroom?

But where are the customs dudes? Now we were not only perplexed but getting a bit miffed at this point.

So we walked into the terminal to do some searching. There was very little activity. It was deadsville.

A small combination gift shop with coffee and snacks. We each grabbed a cup of joe. We then started hearing a lot of noise halfway down the terminal hallway. Like a bunch of guys yelling at a sporting event on TV.

We walked down the hall, all along hoping to spot one of our traveling roadies and/or the customs fellas... We were getting a little concerned about our lost entourage and the Feds.

After venturing a bit down the terminal we soon discovered the essence of the noise and ruckus. The sounds grew louder as we approached the terminal bar. Lo and behold, it was the customs dudes and our roadies, partying together(?)... And they were having what seemed to be a damn good time at it! WTF!? OK.

We walked in to the bar and we were kinda in awe and shock, like, what's going on?

We stepped into the commotion and they all looked up and the roadies went, "Far out, it's our pilots!" Then the government suits go, "Look, it's the pilots!" - "Yeah, yeah, we know, we're the pilots." was my follow-up remark.

We tried to take in the scene as it was quite surreal. Seeing the long hairs mixing with the black suits.

I casually yet somewhat forcefully mentioned to the group having an obviously jubilant time that the weather had broken and we'll want to determine our customs disposition as soon as possible so that we might get our aircraft up in the air and enroute soon.

One of the customs suits looks up from the bar table and goes... "Michael, you're all set! Here's the signed-off paperwork for your customs clearance... good to go!"

OMG, ok, cool... wtf just happened?

The custom guy continues to mention, "Yeah, you're not gonna believe this." He points to one of the roadies and says, "He went to elementary school with one of my kids and they played in Little

League baseball together."

"Well that's cool" was my lame remark.

As it turned out their dads knew each other from many years in the past and they were enjoying a great, good old boys, reminiscence.

Flashback: LOL... Episodes like this you absolutely learn to appreciate the little odd and simple turn of events that can make your life an absolute pleasant and interesting trip!

After a few more minutes of chuckles and a couple more quick life stories, and upon finishing their drinks, we gathered up all the roadies and headed out to our ship.

Pre-flight accomplished, customs approved, and our flight plan secured, we walked onto the plane just cracking up going, "Can you believe what just happened?" Yes, synchronicity is a great thing.

We cranked up the turbines, taxied the aircraft out, and took off toward our next destination. One final fuel stop planned along the way.

The refueling in our newest location, Cheyenne, WY (CYS) was uneventful. Our departure for CYS would place us into OAK around 9:30pm local. Now thirty minutes ahead of our last scheduled arrival. A long day but still inside the timeline of getting er' done.

Yet, to add to the already turned events, one more episode remained.

Smoke and Lightening...

Just like last-minute changes the backstage offers up at gigs with sound not working right or other such situations, you just never know what might get dished up to you while flying an aircraft. You hope for smooth and uneventful flights every time. Most of the time they are, but some episodes do pop up now and then.

Now on our final leg from the CYS fuel stop enroute to our OAK (Oakland west coast) destination.

Approaching the Utah border, we notice on our flight radar some more weather activity over the Wasatch mountain range. No, not as severe as a squall line as we experienced back in Illinois, but many large thundercells none the less. Oh man, you'd think we had enough bad weather and events for the day, but no.

However, this time we witnessed some openings in the T-cell line that allowed us to pick our way through these weather build-ups. Doing our best to make sure the ride for our passengers was as smooth as we could manage.

Crack!!! A tremendously loud snap sound starboard side of the craft.

I happened to be looking out the right window of the ship, my starboard co-pilot side, and Boom!... Lightening goes through the wingtip onward to the ground. Woah!

Now, I've been in aircraft with lightning strikes all around you, but the experience of having your aircraft struck by a bolt of lightning isn't always common, yet it does happen. Quite the thrill and also concerning.

Well, normally an airplane survives lightning strikes without any major damage. And it appeared just after the hit that we didn't suffer any impairment.

However, when a bit of smoke started rising in the cockpit, that event obviously left us with a slight dilemma, to say the least.

Smoke in an aircraft is not a pleasant sight. As if our day wasn't full enough to this point.

The captain and I started to determine what was wrong. I noticed right away that our radar was now very erratic. Its screen was going in and out and was showing signs of shutting down. We did a quick determination of the radar's circuit breaker location and pulled it to the off position.

The air immediately cleared of the bit of haze in the cockpit. The lightning strike had indeed rendered the radar inoperative. By closing off the circuit breaker the smoke immediately stopped.

Lucky for us we broke out of the weather and the route charts and flight followed by the center assistance on the ground verified that no more weather lay ahead, all the way to Oakland.

Man, what a long strange trip this venture this day had been.

Explanation of Lightning Strike on Aircraft

https://flyingrocksbook.com/xUi

It was very comforting to finally see the welcoming city lights of San Francisco and our Oakland destination just to the northeast. A long day indeed.

The roadies were, funnily enough, well-rested, having slept through most of our flight. Except for the lightning crack which got a bit of their attention – lol.

Upon ramp arrival at OAK, we contacted the corporate owner of the aircraft to alert them that they had a few 'squawks' on their ship that needed to be handled and they'd need to send out their crew to Oakland to attend to the repairs (squawks) before the next flight back to its original home location of Denver.

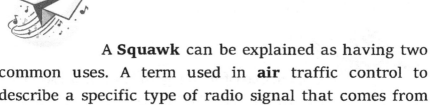

A **Squawk** can be explained as having two common uses. A term used in **air** traffic control to describe a specific type of radio signal that comes from the **plane's** transponder. And a way to report problems with an airplane.

As for my hired captain and myself, we needed to get some decent rest at a local hotel and later secured ourselves some airline flights back to our home lives. They ever desired to be back home again after this endeavor... Ah, the life flying rock!

The **Combi** aircraft idea worked good for this particular Nazareth tour, simply because it concentrated on combining both, the road and stage crew, with the backline and FOH (Front of House) gear, traveling over great distances in a short period of time. However, over time, as I've tested it a few times with bands, the practicality of having everyone fly at once with the gear for routine tour dates never really made sense.

You see, the crew with the gear needs time to set up well in advance of the band showing for sound check, let alone the gig. As such, the conflicting schedules caused more complications than it was worth. It turns out, for national city to city movements, it works best to have the crew move with their own schedule with the gear and the band to have its own transportation to subscribe to their own travel times.

Iron Maiden in the days did make a bit of use of a Combi aircraft for all of their entourage, both, band, crew and gear, for their International endeavors. But these were long hauls where they stayed in one place for numerous concerts before moving on to the next distant destination(s).

Example of Iron Maiden's Combi Aircraft for Int'l flights - Ed Force One

https://fb.watch/cg8TIJoSZ6/

Oakland Stadium July 4, 1979 - Nazareth

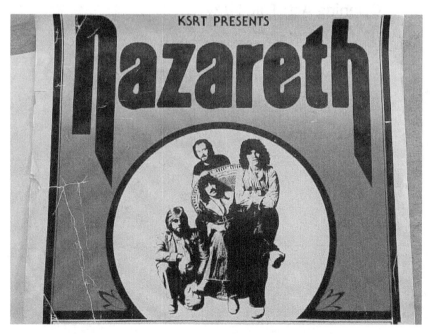

My Memoriabilia Poster

Nazareth Set list for 1979 World (for this) Tour:

1. Telegram, Parts 1-3
2. Razamanaz
3. I Want To (Do Everything for You)
4. Just to Get Into It
5. No Mean City, Parts 1 & 2
6. Simple Solution, Parts 1 & 2
7. May the Sunshine
8. This Flight Tonight
9. Beggars Day
10. Kentucky Fried Blues
11. Born to Love
12. Hair of the Dog
13. Expect No Mercy
14. Love Hurts
15. Shapes of Things
16. Shanghai'd in Shanghai

Opening Act: Thin Lizzy

The Oz Bros' Jet

Many times my phone would ring with potential work and I would have no idea where the caller got my references. This time in the late '80s, an attorney (we'll go with Mr. D.) representative for the Osmond Family was calling to inquire about an aircraft investment. I also later learned that this attorney was instrumental in starting the IMAX theaters.

On this call, he wasn't representing Donny or Marie, but as a legal agent (not to be confused with an entertainment agent) for the Osmond Brothers. I hadn't known such a group of family members ever existed, but I soon learned more about them as our relationship expanded.

The Osmond Brothers consisted of Merrill, Wayne, Alan, and Jay.

https://flyingrocksbook.com/8TU

Mr. D. was looking for a smaller private jet aircraft that would accommodate touring schedules for the O'Bros, along with other management requirements for transportation. Also at that time, aircraft investments offered very aggressive tax incentives if used correctly. An accelerated tax write-off was a part of their inquiry and interest.

It was asked if I would put together a sales proposal for a suggested jet to handle this request. I recall that the market at that time for used jets was offering some decent selections with very accommodating price structures.

After some deep research, I found an appropriate jet for their flight resolution. I was on the phone for hours hunting down options and deals.

BTW, in the aviation industry (back then at least), you really needed to cover your ass by not exposing your client, or even hinting who they are, since many (let's make that most) aviation salesmen representing aircraft organizations would go around your ass in a NY minute. Yep, it was a f*ckn cut-throat av-biz world out there. OK, yet, I've certainly dealt with good many straight-shooting sales folk indeed.

After digesting all of the requirements handed down by Mr. D. and the Brothers Oz regarding all their air travel needs, and after exhaustive research of the best aircraft type and operating expenses for their criterion, I located a small jet at the best competitive price... I discovered and offered them an IAI 1123 Westwind Jet. An earlier offspring production line of the original manufacturer, Aero Commander.

These were the years of transitioning between turbo-jet and turbo-fan aircraft. Most all of the the turbo-jet equipment were still allowed to land at most all airports. They were the best buy on the marketplace at that time.

Osmond Brothers Westwind 1123 Aircraft

https://flyingrocksbook.com/4JA

As a later production pure jet engine propelled ship, the pricing was good on this aircraft. Meaning, it was at the tail-end of an era of allowing very loud straight-pipes, as our aviation industry called them, to continue to operate out of most airports. Also known as, Stage 1. Due to ongoing noise restrictions at certain airports, the next engine stages II & III were known as high-by-pass (turbo-fan) jet engines, which would be quieter than the earliest straight-pipes. Also, stages II and III engines allowed for better fuel economy.

Straight-pipes and high-by-pass fan jet engines

https://flyingrocksbook.com/OXS

By the way, if you're considering buying a jet or turbo-prop aircraft for personal or business use, It's suggested that you first charter for a while. Discover how each of those airplanes feels to you. To start, chartering is even recommended over Fractional ownership. It's a much easier and less expensive way to determine the best aircraft for your needs, without getting locked into costly overhead contract fees.

Since the O's were going to use this jet in airports that still allowed for straight pipes (turbo-jet) activity, they opted to look into the Westwind 1123.

Operating out of my home office attic space in Big Bear City, I remember staying up all night compiling a proposal with printed text/copy and pictures, etc., for the Osmond aircraft deal. It was way back before digital presentation via your computer was even available. Back then it was cut with scissors and physically past together a layout, before having it spit out from a copier and cobbled together in a spiral binder presentation.

Just after the sun rose that very next morning, having not slept a wink, I finalized the completed jet sales proposal. I rinsed off in the shower and rushed to my FedEx office to get the package off by 10 am. Back then the FedEx person did not show up at your door, as it required that you go to their office to send and fetch any such documents.

The jet proposal was delivered the next day. Not long afterward I received another call from Mr. D. Saying that they liked what I sent them. The next thing they requested was for me to meet them at their Utah office.

At their expense, they flew me to their Ogden location. Within a week after that first phone call, I sat across the table from Merrill Osmond, in their Ogden, Utah, recording studio and offices.

I recall the time spent in the Ogden UT hotel during my aircraft negotiations with Merrill and the Oz Bros. On the first night of my arrival, I met Merrill to chat a bit. I remember going downstairs to meet Merrill in the hotel lobby and noticing that he was surrounded by a swarm of lady fans. Talking with him and asking for his autograph (all that show-biz stuff). Being in the entertainment industry, this scenario played itself out for most all of the stars that I've flown. I always found it fascinating.

Entertainers discovered many moons ago the value of private aircraft transportation, which allows for private and secure travel.

Merrill was a really nice dude. He and his brother, Alan, just loved to chat about gathering further information about the Westwind Jet and the private aviation industry. We talked about which airports they would normally fly in and out of for their touring appearances.

In my humble opinion, I had quoted a decent price for the jet. I knew it was very competitive in the marketplace and besides, I was sitting in their office at their request, which meant they had a vested interest in the plane and working with me.

Westwind Interior

Near the end of our conversation about the Westwind, a little (large) bombshell was tossed my way.

I had assumed (never assume) that the Osmond Brothers had decent banking power and figured they already had a fiduciary relationship to secure the purchase of their soon-to-be jet. Now, they may have had such a relationship, yet, Merrill and Mr. D. (who was on the office conference line at that meeting) asked me the surprise question... "Michael, we want this jet. It's what we need for our travels, only one thing... Do you have aviation financing available?"

"mmm wtf!?" talking internally to myself, "The boys don't even have financing available for the purchase of this bird?"

...Oooops, a slight hiccup.

I didn't have an immediate answer for the finance question just tossed my way. In my mind I was a little down, thinking (to myself) O'shit, I just flew many hundreds of miles on the assumption this deal was on the rails to be delivered, only to have a side rail slip-up present itself.

Now, it wasn't like I hadn't been down many roads in the aviation business that presented problems to be tackled. Even though I wasn't prepared and didn't have a banker for this deal in my back pocket before sitting down at the Osmond office table, I just felt and knew I could put something together (lol!... Was I being a bit cocky with myself). Then in hindsight, it might have been a smart idea to at least have a couple of finance options in my pocket before my venture to the O's office. Too late for that now. Time to think on my feet.

I said, "Let me get back to you on finance options. We should be able to swing something that will assist with your resolve to secure the airplane you desire." (I tossed in the word 'desire' as emotional marketing verbiage – Oh boy, here we go).

On my flight home from the Osmond location, I pondered my latest dilemma. If I were to sell this aircraft, I needed some banking money as fast as possible to keep this train on its rails... Or is that, keep the plane on its flight path? Mmm, anyway...

Having no idea how to handle the financing for the Jet during this period of my life, right after my return to my humble, hot, and musty luxurious Big Bear City 'attic' office (with old-school pull-down access staircase), I decided to forget about it the rest of the day.

As it happened, that same night was my monthly (penny-anti) poker game with some of my local neighborhood dude friends. Later that evening, during a dealer's choice round, a poker bud of mine at the table asked me where I went off for a couple of days. I briefly explained the Osmond Brothers' endeavor. And further mentioned the finance hiccup. After a few hours at a poker table, especially after a few elbow tips, you tend to loosen up with conversations. (hehe)

Another player at the table immediately spoke up and mentioned that he lived next door to a banker whom he communicated with a fair amount, and if I was interested he'd introduce me to him about my project.

I remember thinking upon my poker table associate's mention of his banker friend that, no way in hell is his banker neighbor going to know or be interested in loaning money for an aircraft. No way!

But, I looked up from my hand of cards and remarked to him, "Sure, if there's an opportunity to speak to him, that would be cool." And left it at that.

A couple of days passed while researching and creating a short list of finance banks and companies that had aircraft loaning experience, where I would call and pitch the deal. I then received a phone call from a person providing his name as a neighbor and bank friend of my poker player associate. He was interested in the Osmond jet loan. Thinking to myself, Really?

It was indeed a call I never expected, this caught me a bit off-guard, but eh, go with the flow.

He was curious how they would go about working with the Osmond Brothers and the aircraft I had secured for them. The banker wanted to know how to obtain more info on the situation. I suggested I'd drop off the aircraft purchase proposal to his bank since it was just an hour's driving time away from my living quarters.

The banker mentioned that once received he'd get back with any further follow-up requests and details. So, off I went to deliver a copy of the same jet proposal I sent to the O's.

Within a day of dropping off the aircraft sales proposal, that banker actually called and said he'd FAX me a list of requests to continue with the loan for the jet. Which he did within minutes of our conversation. At that time it was your typical loan request. From what I recall, it was the last three years of tax statements, balance sheet stuff, and corporation details, along with a few other related questions regarding how they had planned to use the jet. Nothing out of the ordinary. I forwarded it to Mr. D. for his further distribution to Merrill.

Within 48 hours of my conversation with the banker, hence sending the loan package requirements, this bank called me back (did I mention they were a Savings and Loan?) and mentioned that they indeed had started to receive paperwork from the Osmonds. Really? "Cool," was my (lame-ass) response.

Now all of a sudden it appeared that the jet deal was back in the air again! Timing can be everything!

It was a good thing since the seller of the jet was wondering if I was still interested, as he had another buyer in the wings (pun intended), but I had the first option for the week I had gathered (or stumbled into) the closure of a sale. Like many, if not most business deals, it's a dance! But now the pressure builds a bit more.

Up to this point, I found and introduced a biz-jet to the Osmond Brothers, located initial (pending) financing, and negotiated a fair price from the seller. The middleman [me] in this instance made it happen. I didn't have any reservations about securing my cut of the aircraft to secure a final price for the O'Bros and the bank.

Another few days passed, knowing that some additional documents were pending from the O's office to be delivered to the bank, I was still in the research mode and making ready a short list of possible backup financing institutions, pending the go or no-go from the Savings and Loan bank.

Then I got the call I was looking forward to.

The banker goes, "Michael, all the information you forwarded to us looks good at our end, we're ready to finance the jet aircraft you've recommended. When and what procedures are required from you as the broker to secure this transaction?"

Now I'm yelling "Yeess!" out of my hot musty attic office window!

Immediately thereafter a call was made to the seller of the jet, with the subsequent arrangement of paperwork regarding the distribution of funds, transfer of title, et. all.

During finance, I had arranged for the seller to deliver (ferry) the aircraft from its sold location in Dallas to Las Vegas, the staging area for the Oz Bros first departure flight location.

Normally in a straight-up airplane charter consultant deal, I would have the requirement and experience of reviewing all the credentials of crew members, insurance, legal, and accounting, as a part of the overall management of the aircraft offered to the entertainer (or VIP). Usually, the flight crew already worked for and flew the pertinent corporate chartered aircraft. However, in this instance of selling a jet, it went much deeper, a whole lot deeper.

Not only were there requirements for hiring available crew members for this ship (oh boy, more research) but this aircraft required two pilots, captain and first officer, to legally fly. Noting that you can really fly these smaller jets with one pilot. OK, you might have to reach over a bit further to activate the gear-up handle. Later, smaller jets became single-pilot available, but this craft, like many corporate jets in those early days, required 2 certified flight crew members up-front.

Management of an aircraft goes even deeper. Not only does the aircraft require routine scheduled maintenance, but it also requires ongoing major inspections that take place on the aircraft, per flying hour. It requires pop-up major inspections and repairs issued by the Federal Aviation Administration (FAA) called, Airworthiness Directives (ADs), along with other babysitting chores like; sheltering (providing a hangar space), cleaning, and a ton of other shit, that need monthly attention. It's a bitch!

The reason I found myself staying mostly in the charter consultation field, was because the babysitting and managing of ownership of a sophisticated aircraft, like this Westwind jet, is a continuous chore, as opposed to doing charter aircraft consultations, but alas, the charter industry was a bit slow at that time and the Westwind deal would provide me with additional monthly revenue, at least for the time being, as you'll soon discover.

Once their Westwind was secured with the purchase transaction, I was further finding myself acquiring the crew. I spent a fair number of days hanging out around the Vegas airport. (Aside) I didn't (and still don't) care for Las Vegas but I must confess, however, I've met some very [really] interesting characters at the private aircraft operations side of the McCarran Int'l airport. Located on the very other side of the airport, away from the airliners. We have our own private loading and unloading parking section for private aircraft.

BTW, the private airplane parking facility in the aviation world is called an FBO (Fixed Based Operations/Operator).

I remember at that time, while I was waiting and noodling around the airport during those Osmond aircraft days, this guy (name withheld) who owned his LearJet-23 aircraft (the original early corporate jets), was also hanging out a the local private FBO lobby. He was a radical dude. He happened to be an acquaintance of the Hilton Hotel chain BAC-111 corporate jet (airliner type) aircraft operations.

After meeting with this dude, that evening we climbed aboard his LearJet, drank a bit of champagne, and had a great time hanging out on the ramp talking airplanes and music.

This same guy assisted me in starting and running the jet engines on the O's jet, keeping the lubricants up to date. Airplanes like cars don't like to sit idle very long.

Later, he was intent on showing me how cool it was to shoot his 9mm into the Las Vegas desert air from his LearJet hangar location, but that's another off-topic story, not to be included in detail in this book. Not of my doing, but... Boom, boom, boom, into the distance they flew.

The day came when my hired flight crew arrived in Las Vegas to get some air time on the ship. And after about a week they met up with the Osmond Brothers to launch their tour in the jet.

I had the Westwind flying here and there around the USA for numerous Osmond Brothers' appearances.

Then a short couple of years later, after taking ownership, I noticed a tremendous drop in their aircraft use. To the point where the crew was placed on an as-needed basis. This meant they didn't fly the ship enough to require a flight crew to be available full-time, only one-offs very part-time now.

That was a time in our economy when the interest rates for real estate touched 18%! (remember those days?). It was also a time when the entertainment touring industry took a bit of a hit. Less touring meant less use of the airplane for the O-Bros. As well as many of my other entertainment clients' charter aircraft gigs. The Westwind jet began to sit more and more. Not good for an airplane to sit and not fly for extended periods.

I secured the aircraft with all the required engine inlet and outlet protection plugs. Covered the sensitive exterior holes like the pitot tube and static ports, along with windows, and tire protection.

The ship sat for many months. Sad, since along with this, my monthly management revenue also dried up. Their payments went a bit south you might say. The entertainment industry was suffering. Yes, there have been many pre-Covid hits in the industry.

Many months after the aircraft had been parked and stored the lender [bank] on the jet called. I wasn't in the office at the time of their call. At this point, I hadn't worked for the Osmond Brothers for almost a year. I remembered it probably meant they were wondering about the aircraft. It went even further than that, however. The bank called to let me know that they would be re-possessing the aircraft... Oh boy, I knew something like this might happen, and now was the day.

The economy and touring industry dried up enough to discontinue payments on the ship, now many months in arrears. I remember a lot of touring acts hitting the skids at that time. So, it really wasn't out of the ordinary for small entertainment corporations to adjust their fiduciary directions.

FLASH BACK *I'm reminded of a couple of downturn years in the entertainment travel industry during the same time that the Oz Bros took a hit. The touring charter consultation industry dried up. While waiting for the tours to pick up again, I found myself turning in a different aviation direction. I started building aircraft hangars for rent. I did this for a couple of years. Then the touring industry kicked into gear again.*

The shocker came when the banker asked me not only if I could move the aircraft to a different location during the repossession process, it was further asked if I would sell the airplane. Normally, this would be a great deal to pick up the back end and re-sell the same piece of (aircraft) equipment. But the rub here was the fact that this aircraft had sat for almost a year and needed a bunch of maintenance and, in the meantime, the pure-jet industry took a major nose dive in value. Remember, this wasn't a newer fan-jet-type ship.

I recall thinking to myself that the bank wasn't going to be very happy with me when I told them that the value of the plane would be less than half of what they loaned on it. Oh shit.

I guess the marketplace and economy across the board worked in my favor, for the bank said they didn't care how much the aircraft lost in value, just sell it for whatever they could get for it.

Phew, wiping sweat from my forehead. It appeared that banks also like write-offs – hehe, LOL!

I subsequently got the bank to cough up enough bucks to get the required Westwind maintenance items up-to-date. In the meantime, I offered the aircraft for sale on the marketplace. Shortly thereafter a sales organization in Texas called me and mentioned they had a buyer. And interestingly enough, the offer was only twenty percent less than the original Oz Bros purchase price. Wow, the bank turned out to love me in the end. LOL!

Here's what I learned through this exercise... Synchronicity.

Synchronicity (German: Synchronizität) is a concept first introduced by analytical psychologist Carl G. Jung "to describe circumstances that appear meaningfully related yet lack a causal connection."

Synchro has applied itself much of my life. That is if I've listened at that moment. (LOL/hehe)

Even at a casual poker table, never say never to anything that comes your way, because you never know. And as I learned, making a few bucks on the transactions along the way adds up, compared to chasing a one-time cut of a whole hog.

The business of an independent aviation consultation presented me with times of inspirational accomplishments and yet, at other times it created a very lean bank account. In some instances, I had no idea where my next income flow would develop. Many times Top Ramen noodles were my foodie.

A roller coaster ride to say the least. Yet, I always kept the opportunity of my next client open in my soul. And clients would eventually show up. In business, as you probably know and have experienced, those moments where the breeze is in your face, yet many times the wind is behind your sails all the way.

Banks Won't Fly The Dead!

Generally, as I developed my skills at being a private aircraft consultant, as opposed to actually flying every tour as a pilot myself, the ability to work with high-level brand-name corporations offered a sense of security. I was working with some of the best pilots and airplanes for charter the aviation industry had to offer.

Most of the time these upper-level aircraft flight department operators provided smooth communications. They always provided the proper paperwork that assured all safety measures were addressed before and during my arranged flights for my clients.

On some occasions, some funny or at least entertaining (no pun intended) episodes would indeed pop up.

I'm reminded of an instance when the Grateful Dead had a short tour outing of about a week in the West, which included a departure from their home base in San Francisco to Las Vegas, Phoenix, Los Angeles, and back home.

As a flight consultant, you're always interested in working with folks that operate very nice equipment. Many that I've relied on in the past were the best to work with, especially on a moment's notice.

I always kept a list of backup aircraft that were good flight operations, yet some were unavailable when needed, or otherwise turned down my request to fulfill a charter request due to the clients I worked with.

Rock n' Roll folk by some Corps were considered to be radical. Some of the large corporate flight charter departments seemed confused by the hyper stories of rock stars tossing televisions out of their penthouse hotel rooms... I have never heard of a story of a TV having been tossed from a pressurized aircraft. LOL!

On this particular short (pop-up) Dead itinerary my first choice of planes, which were usually available for charter, weren't. My next resolve was to dig deep into my stand-by list of reliable airplane operators to see if I could sniff out a candidate to handle this tour. On my list of backup charter aircraft for consideration was a very large bank nearest the hub of the Grateful departure point.

My next available best choice of charter aircraft was Denver. Way too far away to make economic sense. The cost to 'deadhead' the airplane between Colorado and a West Coast tour wouldn't work. Essentially paying for an empty aircraft to ferry between the West Coast and Denver.

Deadhead (with the exception of the pun)

https://flyingrocksbook.com/r2o

For over a decade I was attempting to get this major bank's aviation department to take on my request to fly the Dead, however, in every attempt to secure flights for them, this bank would always turn me down. They didn't want to be the aircraft charter operator that had that situation where one of the band members would be first to toss that television out of their jet at 30 thousand feet! (ha!)

I wasn't a big fan of working with banks anyway, but in this instance, I decided to push through in fetching a qualified craft in a very thin marketplace capable of handling this tour.

On this occasion I desperately needed their [this bank's] aircraft or I'd have to go to Denver. I really needed this bank's aircraft to make this Grateful tour work.

My contact for the bank's aircraft was their aviation chief pilot and director of operations. He was a nice enough guy but (again) reluctant to work with me because of my clientele. Being a representative of the bank, he always played the not very interested game when it came to my trouble making rock n' roll hippies.

However, on this occasion, I needed an approach that would have him consider my request. I had spent over a decade trying to break the ice with this bank's aviation department. Now would be the time to do so. So, I pulled out all of the stops.

I still lived in Southern California and had access to numerous small aircraft for utility flights as I needed. The bank was located in the Bay area. A two-and-a-half-hour flight up the coast in one of the puddle-jumping single-engine airplanes I had access to.

In my most recent phone conversation with this bank's chief pilot, I suggested that he at least meet me in person, as a way to get to know each other beyond our decade-long phone conversations. He agreed but noted that it wasn't necessarily going to sway his conviction of (not) flying my rock band.

Grabbing an available small single-engine Cessna 182 aircraft, I flew to Oakland International for my arranged early afternoon meeting with this bank's aviation department.

Upon arrival at Oakland, I arranged for a rental car. In this instance, I rented the best-looking Cadillac that I could find. You'll see why in a moment. I headed over the bank's way.

Now mind you, I still looked somewhat like a hippie with longer hair (long-haired people need not apply... lol). However, I had a few substantial credentials up my sleeve, along with the Caddy look (hehe).

I also knew that by mentioning the fact that I possessed a Certified Flight Instructor (CFI) and commercial pilot's ratings, along with my Federal Aviation Administration Technician Inspector (IA) license, would assist with breaking the ice with this bank's chief pilot.

The first thing the chief pilot asked me was, "What's with the caddy? Don't you Grateful Dead people move around in hippie VW vans?"

At first, I thought he was just being a bit sarcastic or at least attempting a lame hippie joke. I mean, anyone who knows the Dead knows they don't run around in VWs on tour... Or, at least not since the 60s fgs!.

Then after explaining himself further, the chief pilot laughed a bit and assured me that his remark about the VW was just an ice-breaker. Mentioning he had always enjoyed our conversations in the past. He was very impressed that I would take the time to actually fly in a small aircraft and rent a car, just to visit him after all of these years. He immediately opened up to be quite friendly and showed acceptance of my request to work with his banking firm. He genuinely felt that I was sincere about my request to fly the Dead.

Aviation folk tend to spend a fair amount of time telling flight stories, otherwise known as "hangar talk" – chatting about many aviation experiences.

After our ice-breaking conversations, it was time to dig a bit deeper with some serious business. We must have talked for about an hour about past aviation ventures. I now had at least broken ice with the bank guy, with many of my av-career stories matching his.

The chief pilot looked over at me during our discussions and goes, "OK Michael, you've convinced me to look at your request to fly the Dead... Besides, now you've got my curiosity up. After meeting with you and now knowing your background in aviation better, and how much you've shown me the enjoyment you get by providing air transportation for the music industry, let's take a look at your tour requirements, if you're still interested."

"OK" was my simple response.

We looked over the itinerary for the Grateful tour, which blended perfectly with the bank's existing flight bookings. The initial wholesale pricing perfectly aligned with my ability to close this tour with the Grateful accountants. The chief pilot says, "Alright, if you can secure the payments as you described we'll do the tour in our aircraft, but one caveat before we sign the deal..."

I thought to myself, oh shit, one caveat could mean anything... I replied, "And what might that be?"

The chief pilot says, "I'm going to be the one flying as captain on this tour, not one of my other qualified line pilots. You're going to be on my quick dial if anything weird happens with this band."

I'm thinking to myself... geez, this guy is really getting a touch paranoid.

In some cases in the past where I knew that I had other aircraft to choose from for a trip or tour, I would otherwise tell the operator giving me some testy nonsense like this to go pound sand and walk out. But in this instance, I was actually excited to work with this bank, because I knew that after all of these years of resistance and un-called-for bullshit this would be a cakewalk, knowing that the Dead didn't toss TVs out of airplanes.

We finished our business with the continuance of more pleasurable hangar talk.

Immediately after I met with the bank, I headed across the bridge to San Rafael to meet up with the Dead folk at their office. Chatted with a few of the production people prior to the tour launch. Their aviation contracts were always handled directly by their personal Dead Corporation attorney. He resided out of Reno – the Lake Tahoe area... I always did all the legal stuff by phone and fax with him.

I headed back to my So. Cal. Big Bear Mountain home base, knowing that the bank's aircraft was assured for this Dead venture.

The Dead tour was secured by both the bank and the Grateful's legal team, and we were set to depart on their first leg within a week after the contract signatures.

FLASH BACK Back then, the Grateful Dead always answered their office phone line. Mind you, this was way before caller id., so they had no idea who was calling... You'd think they would have answered with, "Grateful Productions", "Bear Productions" or even "GD"... Nope, every time they'd answer their calls with, "Hello."

(hehe, cool eh, loved it!)

Dead Tour Launch Day

The day of departure for the Dead mini-tour arrived. The departure point happened to be from the backyard of the bank's aircraft's home base in Oakland CA. The first leg taking the band to Las Vegas for a couple of concert dates.

I sat in my funky attic home office in Big Bear California, staring at my phone knowingly that I'd be getting a call shortly, just after the first leg arrival in Vegas. And sure enough, the phone rings within minutes of their scheduled landing.

In those days we didn't have caller ID, but I figured it was him. Yep, it's the chief pilot (the captain on this flight and director of operations of the bank) calling. I prepared myself for any number of conversations we'd be having after the first leg of this tour. Including the possibility that the first flight leg didn't go so well. Whatever, bring it on.

"Michael!" I hear the chief pilot with almost a scream in his voice... "Why the fuck did you wait this long to have us fly your Grateful Dead client?" Somewhat (no make that very) perplexed, I asked... "What do you mean?" He goes, "Dude, this is one of the most pleasurable group of folk I've ever flown!"

He continues, "Now I'm feeling a bit pissed at myself for not having worked with you many years ago... You were right, they are a wonderful group to be around. Michael, please accept my apologies and remember, I will never turn you down on future flights knowing that you arranged to fly rock n' roll bands... You've done your best to convince me otherwise!"

Well, they didn't toss a TV or microwave, or whatever out of the plane, HeHe!... Oh man, place a feather in my cap, eh? It only took me over a fuckn' decade to secure this bank's approval.

Note to self: Good story but I still fucking hate banks! (LOL!)

FEDERAL EXPRESS

November 22, 1994

Mike Lofton
Gold Mountain Intercharter
60 Morning Glory Ave.
Durango, CO. 81301

Dear Mike:

Please find enclosed our check representing payment for the two aircraft being chartered for our Denver trips next week, together with the contracts executed by Cameron Sears.

Cameron would really like to get the fully executed signature pages back on Monday if possible. Maybe that could be accomplished by FAX? If that's not feasible, please send them to us as soon as possible.

Thanks.

Sincerely,

Jan Simmons

Enclosures

Grateful Dead
BOX 1073, SAN RAFAEL, CA 94915 • TELEPHONE (415) 457-2322 • FAX (415) 457-9402

This was one of many letters I received from the GD office.

Richard Marx

Record Breaker

In October of 1991, Richard Marx's management got a hold of me with the request to assist with a private aircraft, which would provide a means of moving their band, sound & lights members, and management across the country (USA) to achieve a world record of the most concerts in one day with the greatest distance from east to the west coast. Oooh, a nice challenge indeed.

It had something to do with his album release.

Rush Street

https://flyingrocksbook.com/lfn

I secured the required aircraft (a modified DC-8 back then) and went about arranging the details needed to pull it off.

We launched Richard's record-breaking day starting early morning on November 9th, 1991, with a pick-up in Washington DC. We hit the road early in conjunction with the release of Marx's third album, "Rush Street". He performed a rather early (by rock standards) gig in DC prior to his record-breaking venture.

I worked with a buddy of mine, Mick, an AR fellow over at Capitol Records, along with my associates at MGM Grand Air. By the end of the day, we had subsequently partaken and enjoyed a newsworthy achievement.

This was the Bird

Termed the 'Plug-and-Play' - as the band just showed up and plugged in their instruments and jammed... Did a quick PR FAQ and then off to the next gig. I forgot how long each gig had to be, but I believe it had to meet a minimum of time on the stage to qualify as a concert.

Marx's Itinerary in the U.S. was... DC, NY, Toronto, Chicago, and LA (simple, yet powerful) Flying westward, we were able to gain some hours to complete this agenda, inclusive of all of his flight times, gigs, interviews, and ground time to move to and from the airport. Heck of a way to promote your recent record release, eh? I was a fortunate man to have taken part, indeed!'

I forgot how long each gig had to be, but I believe it had to meet a minimum of time on the stage to qualify as a concert. The itinerary in the U.S. was... DC, NY, Toronto, Chicago, LA (simple, yet powerful)

Flying westward, we were able to gain some hours in order to complete this agenda. Inclusive of all of his flight times, gigs, interviews, and ground time to move to and from the airport.

Interesting way to promote your recent record release, eh?

A fun adventure in the record books.

Jimmy Buffet in Viscounts

Shortly after the Jimmy Buffett Son of a Son of a Sailor Tours, where I flew the Fairchild Cheeseburger F-27 aircraft in '78/'79, I provided the next airplane in line for Jimmy's flights/tours in the early 1980s... The Viscount aircraft. A ship similar to the aircraft I flew the Commodores and Lionel Ritchie's Brick House tour a few years earlier.

The Viscount is a very large 4-engine Rolls Royce turboprop aircraft that wasn't that fast (maybe 260 kts) but could carry a lot of folks and was very roomy in an executive seating layout, and a favorite amongst many touring acts in those days. This particular airplane had 21 seats in living room-style comfort.

Jimmy on the ramp in Burbank So. Cal. USA

In the late 70s and early 80s, I was operating as a sole proprietor under the name, MJL Enterprises. During those times I was living and operating my biz out of Big Bear City Airport in Southern California, and from my humble home attic office. As the eighties progressed, we (my ex-wife and our daughter at that time) migrated to Durango Colorado. I had renamed the business by then to, Gold Mountain Intercharter. Gold Mountain handled aircraft sales and leasings, while Intercharter was the arm that managed most of the subsequent touring aircraft charter arrangements for the entertainers' flights.

I learned my lesson after a few years of using my own (leased F-27) aircraft that maintaining a flight crew and the required maintenance to keep such a ship in tip-top condition on the road took a lot of my earned income. A whole bunch. In some instances, the maintenance expenses totally wiped out all of my profits!

Besides, operating one aircraft limited my abilities to arrange and fly numerous entertainers on tour with overlapping dates. For example, while I was flying the F-27 Cheeseburger aircraft for Buffett, I was approached by numerous other bands to help them with their air transportation.

The problem was that many tours started on opposite coasts of each other, or they did not dovetail into Buffett's existing touring itinerary.

So, I determined at that point that my next resolve would be to get out of the airplane operation (eg., leased ownership) biz and begin the development of a consultation-based service, whereby I would become the middleman for the VIPs and Entertainers, and the companies that owned heavy iron (big turbine aircraft) that needed to charter their aircraft for tax purposes. They had the deep pockets to handle any maintenance requirements.

In so doing I removed the burden of maintaining my own flight crew and maintenance bills. Also, I was able to locate aircraft closer to the bands touring departure points to secure better, equitable price quoting structures.

And, the large corporations that owned the aircraft, of which I would ultimately arrange with to handle these entertainment touring schedules, were liable and responsible for operations and had the deep pockets to handle the ever-rising insurance costs.

Interior of the Viscount

In those days I was called a Charter Broker. I'm guessing the biz is still called that. You might have labeled me as an 'over-glorified entertainment private aircraft travel agent' (OGEPATA). Albeit, arranging to fly the most renowned entertainers in the world, which I guess puts a slightly different spin on that label.

Now, as a 'middleman' for other high-level aircraft owners, and free from the burdens of managing my own ship(s), as a consultant, I was free to take on many tours at once in numerous qualified aircraft.

Aircraft Charter Broker

https://flyingrocksbook.com/2eu

So, what does a OGEPATA consultant do?...

If I wasn't the one flying the birds myself, I'd be strapped to my home office desk juggling tours. eg., negotiating flights in numerous aircraft, insurance requirements, pilot certification verifications, maintenance records reviewed, itinerary landing and parking facility securement details, legal documentation negotiations, accounting, distribution of payments, passenger manifest updates, and ongoing daily communications between aircraft crew and road management personnel. Like calls from the tour manager to verify and/or change certain plans according to weather deviations and venue arrival time changes.

Jimmy's Viscount Flight Deck

Also, Throughout my many aircraft offerings to many entertainers, the Rolls Royce Dart engine was predominately used as their powerplant. The aircraft using the RR were, the Gulfstream 1, the Fairchild F-27, and the Viscount...

History of the Rolls Royce Dart Engine

https://flyingrocksbook.com/oZC

Jimmy's Viscount Ramp Pictures...

So, the evening before Buffett's tour arrived at the Burbank Airport in Southern California, I was hanging out at a bar in Santa Monica (about 30 minutes away). A bit of partying if you will. As the night went on I befriended a guy that was a professional photographer. Remember, before cell phone cameras existed, you needed a high-quality camera to take decent pictures to be a real photographer. OK, professional photographers are still needed.

Anyway, he and I continued to party away.

We then met a nice-looking gal, of which we both had an extreme interest in chasing down (it's an old term) for that eve. Back then I was young and single and ready to rumble. I could tell we would probably need to flip a coin on this one (how cheesy - hehe!).

But then I got to thinking (uh oh). Ding!

I made a deal with that photographer on the spot. I told him that I would make the arrangement and give him exclusive access to the airport ramp parking location at Burbank where Jimmy's plane would land and park. I'd give him the opportunity to take some exclusive pics of JB. He could keep some for his portfolio, yet, I also wanted the images for my files.

He was ecstatic! Yet, I mentioned only one caveat.

I get the girl the evening and he backs off. He thought for a minute and said, "OK, arrange for the airport ramp access, I'm going to Burbank tomorrow to take your pictures"... Hand shake secured.

Aviation and Entertainment Backstage Insights, Encounters, and Shenanigans

It's OK, I'm With The Band!
LOL!

Ask, but just don't tell...

Nowhere is this truer than flying most entertainers and VIPs in chartered private aircraft. Along with the FBO business, where keeping the confidences of clients carries great weight.

My clients deserved confidentiality about their mere presence. Details about their comings and goings, frequency of flight, or any words about their missions were kept to a need to know basis.

Catering to private corporate airplanes, and part of what the aviation industry calls their backstage, is the airport parking facility for private aircraft, known as a Fixed Base Operator (FBO). It's where we situated our aircraft for fueling and overnight stays. The FBO is mostly located well away from commercial airline operations.

Fixed Base Operator - FBO

https://flyingrocksbook.com/Map

What clients do when you fly them on their nickel is their business alone. They came to me with the same expectation of privacy expected of a doctor, lawyer, or clergyman. All it takes is one slip for the public and paparazzi to swarm, not to mention the possibility of inhibiting the client's safety. Making the whereabouts known of a high-profile person or band is an open invite to, kidnappers, thieves, and the like.

The most obvious penalty for unwarranted indiscretions is contract termination; one slip and you'd lose their business along with your goodwill.

I learned that keeping clients' confidence demanded little more than a few common-sense basics. No talking out of school. Knowing about where, when, and to whom you speak of a client. An awareness that what you hear can only hurt if you repeat the sensitive information to someone outside the group who needs to know. At least, until after commenting can have no impact.

You never knew where an errant name-drop might lead, even within the FBO environment, where folks should know better. Sure, insiders say, it's all right to ask about a celebrity client; just don't tell.

LOL, the chapter on Guns N' Roses expounds on this example.

As a further example, my flight crew called ahead to an FBO with our arrival with instructions regarding our, ETA (estimated time of arrival), RON (remain overnight) hotel requirements, Fueling and catering needs, along with the next day's departure time.

At the end of our conversation with the FBO, we mentioned that our famous celebrity loved meeting the public - just not at his plane, at the FBO, or hotel, and particularly not without warning.

Well, in this instance, the word started to spread shortly after the manager handed off the communications task to an assistant who promptly took a seat at the FBO lobby desk to handle the task assignments. The assistant mentioned out loud to the facilities line parking and fueling crew employees of the star's arrival.

Not realizing it, a few people in the lobby overheard the mention of the inbound star by name. Apparently, some of these folks who overheard the assignments from the lobby rang up some friends.

Without our knowing, within minutes a small throng of peeps started to grow in the FBO, many of them obviously acquainted. The manager noticed the gathering. He asked repeatedly if he could help the ones that seemed out of place in his lobby. One of the throngs finally answered, "Yes, you can tell us whether [the Star] is on time."

Quick like a decent FBO manager thinking on his feet, while looking back at his assistant at the desk with some alarm, he replied calmly, "Oh, I'm sorry, but it appears that their airplane will be delayed until tomorrow." And to be on the safe side, the manager asked, "Was [the Star] expecting you?" The answer confirmed the worst. "Oh, no, we just heard [the Star] was coming here and we came out to see in person."

The discouraged crowd turned and left the premises. The lobby returned to its usual calm, near-empty norm, scant minutes before our aircraft turned onto their FBO parking ramp.

The manager had a decent talk with his assistant to draw attention to how the whole scene was preventable. Reflecting on the premise that it's all right to ask about a celebrity client; but just don't tell, at least out loud!

Ah, the psychology of discretion while touring with big shots. (hehe)

Being Backstage

Hanging out backstage, you quickly learn that is has numerous levels of access. Generally, the first level is where you get to sit on stage left or right on chairs or bleachers, with minimal access to any other areas. The second level usually consists of maybe getting to the catering location and a general schmoozing section for idle chat of non-essential and some essential individuals. The third (and deeper) level backstage area is the access to dressing rooms and the green (pre-show) room, where only entertainers and direct high-level personnel have entry. Usually, my access badge allowed entry into all of these backstage levels.

Being drunk or high backstage was never a good plan. Especially if you were a part of the aircraft crew. Maybe a glass of wine or two, but the word would travel quickly if you became too tipsy. We didn't need any gossip about, "Hey, did you know that the pilots got pretty fucked up on all those rum and cokes?" Not good.

Backstage Spinal Tap clip - Hello Cleveland

https://flyingrocksbook.com/RNU

... It's OK, I'm with the band [LOL!]

Here are just a few story-lines used by folks who tried to gain backstage access to a concert. I'm sure it continues today.

You probably know a few yourself, eh?

* I'm the guitar player's wife/girlfriend. (pretending to be)
* I'm sure I'm on the backstage list, check again.
* A fan disguises themselves as a band or crew member.
* Fake backstage passes.
* Pretending to bring in equipment (eg., guitar case, amplifier) to act as though they are a crew member.
* Pretending to be a journalist and/or photographer from a famous entertainment magazine or as a podcaster, et. al.
* Trying to slip inside an unmanned door to the backstage area.
* Schmoozing the backstage security person with coffee and dough-nuts.
* Pretending to be a part of the opening act.
* The VIP event planner poses as a coordinator, claiming to have organized an exclusive post-concert party.
* A long-lost relative that has some vital information to pass on to a band member.
* Pretending to be a high-level music entertainment industry person that was requested to be at the concert to hear the band.
* Pretending you left your access pass back at the hotel.
... on and on and on... LOL

Heck, I even had a gal next to me while we waited for backstage access after a concert who tried to convince me that she did image edits for album covers to remove wrinkles from Jimmy Buffett's face... It didn't work. And this was way before digital Photoshop apps were even available.

And, if you're trying to get on the plane, even being the co-pilot's wife didn't work out very well. Check out the Heart chapter.

The airplane was a sacred space. If someone had been invited aboard by band members or road management, they'd been specifically selected as a special person. Even the time one, named the "Gobbler" rode along. But, I'll leave that meme up to you to figure why this person had access for a flight.

Hey, can you do me a favor? (pet peeve!)

So, numerous times someone would ask of me, knowing I flew major rock bands around the country, "Can you do me a favor and..." The list of requests ranged from stupid to pretty funny.

These requests would run the gambit. Like... I have a song that I just know would be perfect for this band. Or, I have some song lyrics that your entertainer would need for their next album. WTF? And the shit folks asked to be delivered backstage. Cakes with the band's image plastered on them. Requests for autographs on bras and panties. The list went on and on.

I got used to these inquiries, and had the pat answer... "Sorry, I don't get involved with my client's business beyond my duties as their private aircraft consultant." I never asked favors from my clients in this regard, and for sure I wasn't going to pass on requests from others. Even though this was my pet peeve, I subsequently couldn't blame the folks asking me for such favors.

Now, asking for concert tickets was altogether different and most all the time I was only happy to oblige. I always remained on the 'down low' whenever I requested special favors of my bands.

As a diversion, yet keeping with the aviation theme in this book, you might find this aircraft traffic tracker website of interest. Click on any aircraft or airport for a more detailed view of who they are and where they are going. Fun to fool-around at this site.

https://flyingrocksbook.com/jcJ

Emmylou's room...

Not that it's a big deal, but while on the road with Jimmy Buffett and the Coral Reefer Band, one evening at the hotel just before heading out to the venue, Jimmy handed me a black acoustic guitar and said... "Lofton, do me a favor and run this guitar down to Emmylou's room." So, I took it over to her room, knocked on her door, and after she opened it I just handed the guitar over and mentioned that Jimmy wanted this delivered. She said, "Thank you Michael" and that was that. Like I said, no big deal but eh, in a way it's a relative short story.

The inception of Acid Rock?

BTW... A curious reference to the inception of acid Rock n' Roll (hint: it actually started in LA not SFO)... Dave McGowan's - Weird Scenes Inside the (Laurel) Canyon lays out some insightful and kinda spooky details. One day I visited the store at the base of the canyon and met a couple of dark (energy) dudes interested in my flying bands. Got chills and headed out of there immediately.

https://flyingrocksbook.com/er9

Comic Relief

Hint, you'll need to be a seasoned pilot to appreciate.

Dan Fogelberg

https://flyingrocksbook.com/QLF

Back in the late 1980s Dan Fogelberg and Jimmy Buffett contributed to our family move to Colorado.

Dan Fogelberg used to live in Pagosa Springs, Colorado, which is located about an hour away from my town in southern Colorado. For more than twenty years, my wife at that time, along with our two children, lived in Durango, Colorado.

Article re: Dan's death 12/17/2007 (just 56)

https://flyingrocksbook.com/tFF

Dan had the same managers as Jimmy Buffett, Irving Azoff, and Howard Kaufman, of Front Line Management. I flew and arranged for Jimmy's tours in airplanes for many years from '78 to '91 working with Front Line.

Front Line also managed the Eagles and a bunch other monster entertainers. Front Line secured Fogelberg's contract with Columbia to have Joe Walsh produce his successful Souvenirs album in '74.

Before moving to Durango, CO from our Big Bear Lake locale in southern California in the late 80s, my then-wife, along with our young daughter, spent time traveling via small airplanes throughout the Southwest US.

On one occasion we visited Santa Fe, New Mexico for vacation. At that time I had at my disposal numerous small planes from a stable of small aircraft maintenance and flight training clients of mine, which I traded maintenance for flight use. I possessed an aircraft technician license (A & P), an aircraft inspector authorization (IA), and a certified flight instructor rating (CFI), which allowed me to establish trade flight hours for aircraft inspections and flight training.

During our stay in Santa Fe I received a phone call from Bob Liberman, Jimmy Buffett's road manager. They were looking for a small turbo-prop aircraft to fly Jimmy and himself into the Pagosa Springs area for Folgelberg's wedding. I learned it was Dan's wedding to his first wife.

Anyway, just after Bobby requested an aircraft, my wife then asked if we could leave Santa Fe early to visit the southwest region of Colorado, which neither of us had ever seen before.

During that vacation in Santa Fe and after Jimmy Buffett's request, I did some research and hopped on the phone to secure the small turbo-prop for Jimmy's visit to Pagosa Springs.

Upon pulling out the aircraft flight sectional (map) for that area (back in them days we didn't have digital maps, it was paper baby!) I suggested that we visit Durango Colorado on our way back to our home to our So. California mountain domicile. It was located in the southwest corner of Colorado and wasn't but a 40-minute flight. At that time I was using one of my customer's trade aircraft. A Piper PA-32R T-tail Turbo Lance. A six-seat, high-performance, single-engine, retractable gear, craft.

My family decided to head out to visit Durango, the next town over from Pagosa Springs. Little did we know what was in store for us in that town.

To finish up on this story, as it doesn't relate to flying entertainment except for me securing an aircraft for Jimmy Buffett during our vacation for Dan's wedding, we landed at the smallest of the two airports, nearest downtown Durango.

At that time, we had a couple of horses back in California. Upon our Durango Airport arrival, the first question my wife asked the airport attendant was, "How much is a bale of alfalfa hay?" I know, kinda weird eh? Yet, when he responded with $2.50 a bale, while we were paying well over $7.50 in California at that time. She looked at me and said, "Michael, we're moving to Durango!".

And she was right, we eventually moved from Big Bear City California to Durango Colorado within a couple of years hence this visit. Horses, dogs, cats, and all! We ended up living there for almost 20 years thereafter. Our son was born there.

I owe Dan Fogelberg and Jimmy Buffett credit for our move to Colorado. Thank you boys!

Some Other Entertainers and Aircraft Flown
(without deep stories)

A catch-all of bands without deep stories, but remembered as being fun to arrange their flights at that time...
I might have even forgotten a couple!

Almost Flew Elvis... His last *tour*

The Elvis tour was set to launch out of Portland Maine around August 17th, 1977. I was the co-pilot on one of two Viscount aircraft heading out of Burbank Airport a day before the tour started. The Viscounts were used primarily to haul some gear, stage production crew, and musicians.

I did discover that Elvis mostly flew on his Convair 880 Jet, the Lisa Marie. Sometimes one of the Viscounts was dispatched to a diverting airport, to pull fan and press crowds away from where the Lisa Marie would land. Ah, the tricks of the entertainment aircraft trade. (hehe)

Image of Lisa Marie Convair 880 Jet Aircraft

Shortly after departure while heading eastward, we received a message from our home-base requesting that we return to Burbank, our departure point. Somewhat perplexed we contacted en-route flight center to amend our flight plan to return home.

Upon arrival at our home-base ramp, we finally heard the news. Elvis had died and the tour was scraped. I remembered being a bit bummed. Not only because of Elvis departing the planet, but my chance to fly this tour would had been a nice piece in my flight log book. Oh well.

So, as of the writing of my [this] book, a fella by the name of Jimmy, happened to buy one of the old (smaller) Elvis JetStar Jets and converted it into an RV... Funny YouTube vids describing such.

(one of the) Elvis Jetstar Aircraft Converted to RV by Jimmy's World

FLEETWOOD MAC

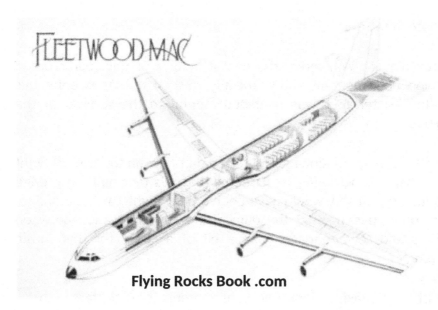

Flying Rocks Book .com

There were a couple of times when I would get a call from a music booking agent looking for a plane for a tour. Yet, they did not need me to manage the flight part of the tour, they simply would hire me to locate a suitable aircraft for their tour, whereby they would assume the responsibility of managing the day-to-day babysitting duties of the itinerary.

In the early part of '80, I was called upon to locate such an airplane for the Fleetwood Mac Tusk Tour. It was, as I recall, for the flight legs that flew in the United States.

Essentially for this project, I was hired to be their aircraft lease broker for what was needed for the Tusk Tour, the second North American legs.

Similar to the Rolling Stones Steel Wheels tour, which I fully managed in a Boeing 720 craft, the Fleetwood Tour would end up in a Boeing 707 executive-configured aircraft that I was able to locate.

The ship had a forward suite-style arrangement with couches, club tables, galley/bar, etc... with the aft portion of the aircraft in first-class seating.

I located the Boeing and arranged to have all of the follow-up paperwork secure via their music agent. Once secured, I was paid a finders fee. No further flight consultation was requested, where in normal circumstances I would be the point man through-out the complete flight portion of the tour for all of their aviation related matters.

According to Wikipedia, the overall length of this tour created havoc, both mentally and financially on the band. Apparently, this roller-coaster tour was near-detrimental to the survival of the group.

In retrospect, I'm kinda glad that I didn't take on the overall flight tour babysitting duties, as it seems that this tour had some edge to it, and probably would have been a daily nightmare to manage. I'm only guessing that the daily flying communication between pilots and road manager was a bit of a stress for that music agent.

I just loved making flight tour arrangements for rock stars in the days... at that time aviation and entertainment retained a wonderful free-lifestyle 'blend' of movement by private air along with the freedom of the continued emergence of original rock music!'

Anyway, it was an experience to get the aircraft located to its tour departure point in Los Angeles. At that time my ex-wife and I flew down from our home in Big Bear California, in a smaller aircraft to inspect the verify that the ship and its crew were ready to go.

Sunshine (ex-wife) and mother of Fawn and Ethan,
in the flight deck of the Fleetwood Tusk Boeing bird.

Paul Simon

Memorabilia tour book

***

Garrison Keillor
W/ Chet Atkins
PBR - Radio *A Prairie Home Companion*

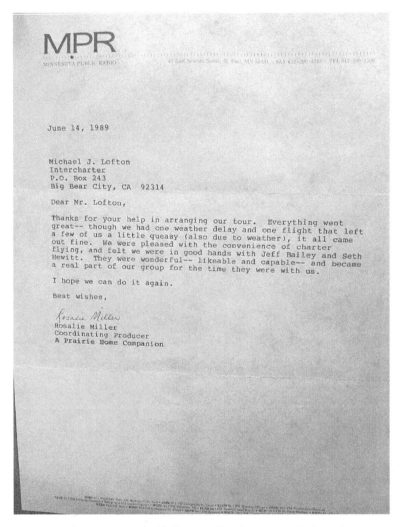

Minnesota Public Radio letter of thanks

Tim Allen - flight into Las Vegas

Got an autographed pic for my Dad, John, who loved Tim

* * *

Lou Rawls Viscount

Viscount interior - Lou Rawls

***

Kings of Comedy Tour

The Original Kings of Comedy was a 2000 stand-up comedy film directed by Spike Lee and featuring the comedy routines of Steve Harvey, D.L. Hughley, Cedric the Entertainer, and Bernie Mac. The film was produced by MTV Productions and Latham Entertainment and was distributed by Paramount Pictures. *(cited from Wiki)*

Most of their tour legs I placed in a Hawker Jet

The actual show was shot over the last two nights of the Kings of Comedy tour with Harvey, Hughley, Cedric, and Mac. The film was a critical and commercial success, with popularity leading to multiple spin-off films.

The comedians gave their take on African-American culture, race relations, religion, and family in front of a large live audience.

One day in the late 90s I got a call from an East Coast production company, Latham Entertainment.

This was close to the end of my aviation consultation career, whereby shortly after 9-11 would mark the time of me winding down my aviation consultation biz.

The Kings of Comedy tour mostly departed from Los Angeles for a few days at a time during years 1999-2000.

In securing this flight contract I communicates with Harvey's tour manager, a nice gal out of Los Angeles. She also was a personal assistant to Steve Harvey. I remember talking with her one day and Steve was in her office at the same time. He gets on the phone and thanks for assisting with the airplane on this important filming tour.

It was kinda funny since Steve also asked me where I grew up. I told him Southern California and went to John Muir High School. He goes, "Muir! Dude you're a white soul brother!".

You see, Muir was a rationally mixed school at that time in the late 60s (I graduated 1970). We witness the smoke burning from the original Watts riots on our school campus. Muir is also known as having the best drum corps in the country with mostly black players.

Muir was also the school where, David Lee Roth, from Van Halen also attended. He was a year or so behind me at that time. More on that in the Van Halen chapter.

Anita Baker

Memorabilia tour book

***

Starship

1987 Tour Memorabilia tour book

Jerry Garcia Band
His band regularly toured and recorded sporadically throughout its twenty-year existence, generally, but not always, during breaks in the Grateful Dead's schedule.

Weir/Wasserman (RatDog)
Spent a little time with Bob Weir, driving him from the Durango CO airport (my home town then) to their gig.

Memorabilia tour book

Huey Lewis & The News

Memorabilia tour pass

- INXS
- Crystal Gayle
- Dionne Warwick
- Lee Anne Rimes
- Engelbert Humperdinck
- Quincy Jones
- Jefferson Starship
- Frank Zappa
-Tim Weisberg
(put my flute on top of the luggage please - hehe)
- Pablo Cruise
- Kenny Logins
- Robin Williams
- Duran Duran
- John Hyatt (flight re: video shoot)
- Ozzy Osbourne

Rod Stewart

Memorabilia tour pass

- Meat Loaf - Bat Out of Hell tour
- Tower Of Power
- Eddie Murphy
- Moody Blues
- Dwight Yoakam
- Amazing Rhythm Aces
- Governor Brown, first time around (letter of thanks)
- Garrison Keiler – MPR (MN public radio) with Chet Atkins (my Dad's Fav.)
Paul Anka (my Mom's Fav.)

***

Ed note: Bob Skilton interview at the Flying Rocks Book Blog, re: bus info and Ozzy's lead guitarist flight death

***

My Favs Bands, then and now...

Loved all the bands I flew, but wish I also had the chance with... *(to name just a handful - also love Jazz)*

- Humble Pie
- Vanilla Fudge
- Mott the Hoople
- Ten Years After
- Led Zeppelin
- Janis Joplin

So you want to be a rock 'n' roll star?
Then listen now to what I say
Just get an electric guitar
Then take some time and learn how to play
And in a week or two
If you make the charts
The girls'll tear you apart
- The Byrds, 1967

156

Heads of State
& Other VIPs
(Suits)

A counter check and having a banker mess with my head

Every once in a while I received phone calls outside of the realm of musicians. The likes of politicians and other 'so-called' VIPs, to handle their private flight needs.

It was a Saturday morning and I get this call from a representative of a Saudi Head of State. This person mentioned my name was referenced by their attorney friend and his entourage was seeking a large corporate aircraft to do many flight legs that following Sunday.

The pop-up request wasn't so unusual, it was the fact that it was to take place on a weekend when banks were closed regarding any funds being transferred. This request came about in the 80s, before the Internet and the availability of instant digital currency transaction capabilities.

At that moment I remember thinking to myself that only one operator of a corporate DC-9 Douglas jet airliner, converted to an executive interior, might be available for last-minute support for this aircraft movement.

After a brief discussion with the Saudi representative, it was suggested that I would attempt to locate the right aircraft for their request. I then further inquired as to how they would pay for this aircraft charter.

Their ability to pay for the trip would come in the form of a counter-to-counter check, which would be sent by the very next available commercial airline flying from their location in New York to my closest airport in Southern California. The airport that handled large airliners was a good 2-hour drive from my mountain homestead.

I wrestled with this aircraft charter request and made a couple of calls to other industry folks I knew to find out if these Heads of State were someone they'd dealt with before. Within a couple of calls to my insider associates, I did get the response that they'd heard that the specific Saudis I mentioned were good for the money but couldn't assure me beyond that. Taking a check on a weekend for a ton of bucks without bank verification still had me feeling a little [a lot] sketchy. Yet something said go for it.

Once I was able to get a hold of the aircraft charter operator they mentioned that they could do the required itinerary for the very next day (Sunday) flights. And in those days my word was good enough to dispatch the [a] plane upon my approval, with payment to be handled the following week. Kinda scary to think I had that amount of power then to dispatch large aircraft on my word only. Mmm.

Shit... Now, I had no idea who these Saudi guys were and I was on the hook if their very large check would be on my shoulders if it bounced. And I'd be big-time dirt in my air charter industry!

Getting back on the horn with the Saudi representative I secured their counter-to-counter check via the airlines and readied myself for the drive down the mountain to retrieve it. It would take hours before the airline arrived and sure enough, once at the airport a certified envelope with my name on it sat waiting for me at the airline's counter.

In the meantime, I'm back and forth on the phone between the Saudis and the aircraft operator going over the flight plans. Pick up here to take there to wait in order to take somewhere else a couple of hours later. Ultimately their movements would have them flying across the US with a few stops in one full day.

That Saturday required a bunch of logistics to secure their Sunday morning New York pick-up.

Checking in with the flight crew the Sunday evening after the flights, the indications were that everything went smoothly on all the flight legs and the Saudi client seemed happy.

One major accomplishment out of the way, now to deal with the funds.

At that time my banker was a golfing associate of mine and the president of our local mountain bank. We'd occasionally venture off to play golf in the local desert. Sometimes even play little pranks on each other. You know, like putting those explosive puffy golf balls in our bags as a gag.

When Monday morning came around I couldn't wait to get to the bank to present the check to my banker buddy. It so happened that he wasn't in his office that morning. So, I left the check with his secretary and ventured off to do a couple of chores, awaiting his phone call.

About an hour later the banker called me and after I told him how the check came about hence the charter I arranged over the weekend, he kinda chuckled and said that I should come back into the bank as soon as possible.

I thought, why does my banker guy sound like there might be an issue with the check?... Now I'm kinda freaking out a little, as I'm bee-linning it back to the bank.

I walk up to his secretary and she mentions that he's on the phone but will be with me shortly. My golfing bank bud opens his office door and says something like... "Lofton, come on in, we need to talk about your check." -Oh boy, what's on his mind, and what's the deal?

He closed the door as I entered his office, and sat behind his desk. He goes... "Dude, did you really take a check over the weekend no less, made out to thousands of dollars, and dispatched an aircraft on your word, while hoping the check was good?" - Me goes, "I did."

Well here's the deal... By this time I'm starting to feel that queasy, uneasy feeling.

Anyway, the banker leans over his desk and goes... "Michael, not only is this check good but the bank that the check is written on is owned by the Saudi you just flew!"

WTF, whoa!

"I didn't mean to have you feel awkward, but as my golfing partner" he continued, "I couldn't help but mess with ya just a bit."

I could have choked my banker friend right then and there, but the instant welcomed relief that all was now cool took precedent.

The next 18 holes were on him!

California Governor Jerry Brown

And speaking of VIPs, politicians also popped up for personal flight arrangements. Here's a letter from the campaign from California Governor Jerry Brown back in the day. You know, the same one that dated Linda Ronstadt. (hehe)

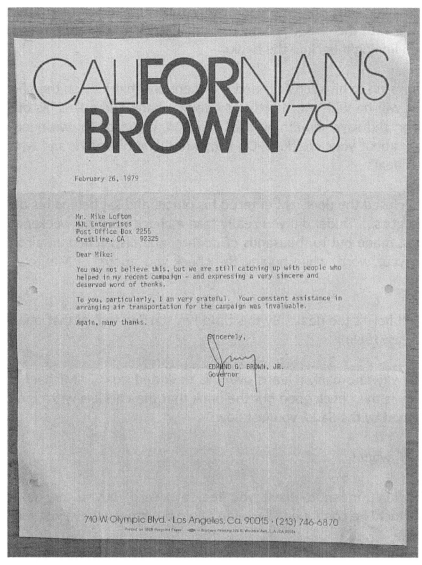

Memorabilia letter

The Bill Graham Episode

Let's talk about the weather and the safety of flying. This flashback hits me pretty hard. You see, Bill Graham was the promoter of all Dead concerts in the Bay area. Back then for his private fixed-wing aircraft and his helicopter, Bill's personal pilot was a guy named, Steve.

Bill Graham - Music Promoter

https://flyingrocksbook.com/Ud9

Once, I attended a music industry production summit conference held and sponsored by Performance Magazine in Palm Springs, California. I was selected as a consultant to sit on their private aircraft touring transportation panel.

At this conference, I ran across Graham's pilot. Never knew of him up to this point. He goes, "Hey, aren't you Michael Lofton?" I go, "That's me." He goes on, "Well I gotta tell ya, man, I had to crack up when you diverted your Grateful King Airs' from Novato Airport last month." He then gets a bit snarky with me. "I know the weather ceiling was low, but you're kinda a wimp to divert your aircraft over to Oakland airport that evening."

OK now I'm wondering what Steve's angle is with his remark. I responded, "So, where is this conversation going?" Steve goes, "Yeah, I was right behind your King Airs' and I made the approach and landed just fine."

The airport, Novato Gnoss Field, was (as of the writing of this book) a smaller airport in Northern California Marin County, where the Dead members lived. Back then Gnoss had what was called, an Instrument Flight Rules circle-to-land approach during low weather conditions. Meaning, you were allowed to descend your aircraft under local cloud conditions, and then proceed to circle around, remaining clear of any additional clouds, to line up with the appropriate runway to land.

Yet, there was the rub that eve with my clients, and the pilots I was directing. I explained to pilot Steve that my King Air crew reported a cloud ceiling lower than was allowed by the FAA (Federal Aviation Administration).

My pilots reported back after their missed approach to ask me via air-to-ground phone communications as to which alternate airport worked?... My response was an immediate diversion to Oakland International Airport. I then had the Grateful Dead ground crew have their limos diverted across the Oakland Bay Bridge to pick up the band members. It was a last-minute hassle, but a safe resolution nonetheless.

Pilot Steve continued his banter. "Well as I said Michael, I made it into the airport right after they diverted."

I knew that Steve flew into Gnoss Field all the time to handle Bill Graham's flights. He knew that area very well, along with all of the hills surrounding this airport, where times in the past some pilots found themselves slamming into them.

Steve continued his rant, "You're still a wimp, Lofton." I go, "Well Fuck You too!" Now, he might have been shuckin' and jivin' me, (as pilots can be persnickety) but he was pushin' a bit hard.

Not trying to be harsh with this flashback, but unfortunately, within a short year after this encounter, pilot Steve, who also at that time went by the name, 'Killer' Steve, flew a bit 'low' in Bill Graham's helicopter, and found some high-tension electrical wires. That was that for Bill and Steve!... Mmm - totally sucked!

Heart

-Barracuda-

The stewardess that didn't belong,
and cardboard notations.

For 13 years, during their heyday from the early 80s through the 90s, I arranged and managed all of the private air transportation flights for the band, Heart, with Ann and Nancy Wilson.

Heart Gulfstream 1 - 1986 (US and Canada) Aircraft

I had many fond memories of working with the Heart sisters and their band members. Over a decade of communicating with their management, attorneys, and accountants. Loved being at the gigs, hanging with their wonderful road/tour manager (at that time), Dick Adams.

For that matter, every one of the road and tour managers that I had aircraft flight arrangements with were unpretentious and also great to work with! They were masters at communications regarding scheduling, and babysitting (aka herding the musician cats). They could juggle many band production members at once.

Difference between a road and a tour manager?

In general, road managers handle tour details for their specific band, while tour managers are used to overseeing the logistics, finances, and communications for tours as a holistic entity.

Tour Manager: https://flyingrocksbook.com/IhJ

Road Manager: https://flyingrocksbook.com/Xnm

One day on the road I mentioned to the road manager, Dick, that it seemed that my days of providing tour planes were dwindling, with the existence of MTV (Music TV). I thought that since most could now just watch live and pre-recorded clips and videos of their favorite entertainers, my days were numbered regarding flying and/or arranging tours in private aircraft. Yet, he assured me that MTV would only increase the want for folks to go out to see their fav band live, and thus my services would indeed be required for many years to come.

Thank goodness he was right, as it turned out that way!

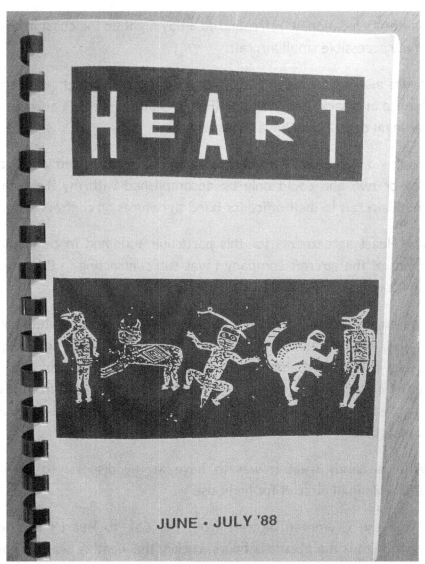

Memorabilia tour book

With my aviation technician credentials, I continued to provide for some small airplane inspections at my local airport, in the mountains at Big Bear Lake California, as a trade for use of air time in small airplanes, which I fortunately, had many small airships at my disposal to shuttle myself out and back from my Big Bear City Airport domicile.

I remember for one tour, an agreement needed to be signed within a day by Heart's attorneys, along with picking up a deposit check from their accountants.

The only problem was the fact that Heart's management and accountant offices were in Seattle. Quite a ways from my So.

California location, which required a day flight up the coast in one of my accessible small aircraft.

It was also a time when FedEx wasn't offering overnight delivery service and back then facsimile (FAX) signatures weren't approved for legal docs. Times have changed, eh?

Unsigned agreements needed to be signed and secured within a day or two and could only be accomplished with my flights in small aircraft to their office for hand signatures on contracts.

The Heart agreements for this particular tour had to be in the hands of the aircraft company I was sub-contracting in Burbank, (in Southern) California, within 24 hours.

I arranged for the use of one of my small aircraft maintenance trades, a Grumman Tiger... A four-place (aka 4-seats) low-wing critter that moved along pretty nicely for its size. Within a few hours, I was topping off the Tiger with fuel and headed from my Big Bear location to Seattle, WA. to handle this Heart tour transaction.

What a handy treat it was to have at my disposal so many different small aircraft for flight use.

Flying the Grumman aircraft from So. Cal. to Heart's Seattle location took me about six hours. Luckily the weather was decent that day. I spent the night in Seattle and blasted back down the coast to Burbank, CA. early the very next day in time for the signed contract drop, along with the deposit check at my subcontracted aircraft company location, which I had arranged to handle this tour. Then it was back to my Big Bear airport that very same day. A full day of flying each way!

The Heart tour commenced without a hitch. One of many over 13 years. However, occasionally some twists and turns would arise...

One of many Heart aircraft interiors

Where Did This Flight Stewardess Come From?

One day while doing a tour consultation, I got a weird phone call from Heart's Road Manager. He usually checked in daily, yet something in his voice seemed a bit harsh on this occasion. Normally in a very professional and comforting mood, this call had a different tone.

He asked me why, after a few weeks on the road, they all of a sudden now they had a flight attendant on board. He got my immediate attention.

From day one of this tour we did not have nor did the band ever request or need a flight attendant. So, besides thinking to myself, wtf!, my curiosity further asked, "Just to make sure, might this stewardess be a part of the Heart entourage?" He goes, "Absolutely Not! We thought you arranged it, Michael."

Oh shit, mmm, (again) wtf!? This was beyond me. I've been tossed some weird questions from road managers, management, accountants, lawyers, etc., over the decades of flying rock but this was one of those oddball types. Since this tour was due to finish in a couple of days the timing also seemed beyond strange.

Now, a flight attendant (or stewardess) wasn't required for many mid-sized touring aircraft, like the G1 secured for Heart on this tour.

Sometimes a stew was requested and we accommodated a certified person to handle the catering and the distribution of food and drinks during flights, along with all the safety considerations. However, as mentioned, no attendant was assigned to this tour.

History of the Flight Attendant

https://flyingrocksbook.com/VPJ

Bands hired me to secure air charter flights to avoid fawning fan contact and autograph seekers. An unexpected addition to the aircraft cabin would add a ton of bad chemistry to the trip. A mismatch that clients should not have to tolerate.

In this instance, I was sub-contracting with a one-man Gulfstream charter provider out of Los Angeles. Hence, getting off the phone with the road manager I immediately called the captain of this ship at his hotel.

"John" (not his real name) "Can you tell me what you know about a stewardess being on the Heart aircraft on your flight leg today?" John goes, "Oh yeah, I was going to ask you later today to see if it was ok with you." I go, "You mean, to see if it was ok with me to place a foreign body in the cabin with a high-profile client without my approval first?" He goes, "Oh man, you don't sound very happy about it."

This wasn't going to be a pleasant conversation for sure. I always hated when conflicts came up with aircraft operators. This was a crappy humdinger!

The captain starts to explain an absolutely ridiculous description of what happened. I'm usually pretty patient with pilots, but this day it was time to blow patience out the window.

The captain went on to explain that the co-pilot's wife was a big fan of Heart. Newsflash, a lot of wives were big fans of Heart (rock stars for that matter! FGS!). Anyway, part of the stop along the tour route (the last airport) happened to be in the city where the co-pilot and his wife lived. The captain went on to explain that the wife was adamant about providing her (free) services and assistance as a stew on their next leg...

So I ask the cap, "How the fuck did the co-pilot convince you to go along with this lame-brain plan?"

The captain tried to explain that it worked out ok and the (Heart) girls didn't seem to mind... OMG, this isn't going to be a nice call for sure! And, I'm not even sure how she got by the road manager. I'm now getting really pissed.

I continued my chat. "Are you fucking kidding me, John? I've run across some pretty bone-headed moves before, but this one percolates to the top."

There was no stopping my rant of horror at this point.

I went on to explain to the captain that I'd be lucky to keep my position as Heart's sole private aircraft consultant after this lame-ass move. I further reiterated and noted that we never place a strange or non-related body in the same cabin as the passengers without prior permission, never! Exclaiming more, "You as the captain should know this rule." continuing, "And of course, this means never ever letting a fucking groupie on the plane for a flight, ever FGS!"

By now the captain was catching my drift.

We had a few more days of touring and I needed to get this situation squared away, pronto. I also needed to get back on the phone with the road manager to smooth out the sails at that end.

So continuing my dialog with the pilot, "Captain John, here's what you'll want to do right after we get off the phone. You call your co-pilot and tell him that if he wants to keep his flying position for the rest of this tour, he'll need to do a few things." I then rattled off the criterion to proceed with the next flight", which was to take place the next day.

"First, tell your co-pilot's wife to get on the next commercial airline flight back home. She is not allowed to be anywhere near the pilots at the private aircraft terminal ramp for Heart's next flight. I want her gone from the scene, today, pronto, period!"

Next, I told the captain, "Make sure that you and the co-pilot explain and apologize to the road manager directly before their next flight. Also, that Mr. Lofton [me] didn't know and was not privy about this situation, as you've learned that it was a stupid call on your behalf."

Then finally, now being exhausted with our conversation, "You better hope I don't lose this account due to your slip-up, or as they say in the music industry, I'll make it hard for you to work rock n' roll ever again!"

Noting that I was a hard-ass back in them days. Besides, I always wanted to use that line. (hehe!)

The captain caught my drift and handled all of the outlined details promptly.

It took me the rest of the day to calm down. I continued to spend time on the phone with Heart's road manager to explain the bone-headed situation. Very lucky for me, I had many years under my belt with him, and subsequent to our conversations and at the end of it all, we each ended up having a decent laugh over it. Each of us knowing how stupid and silly fans can get.

The remainder of the tour went very smoothly. The co-pilot's wife got her moment around fame, but she also got to experience how being backstage, where she didn't belong, developed into a hard-learned lesson about how the rock and the aviation biz works.

Oh, the pain of going through this ordeal, dealing with a hand full of sub-contracted charter organizations and their pilots.

BTW, I never worked with that flight organization again, due to this wacky episode. OMG, the lessons learned in this industry.

Cardboard Notes for the Heart

In the late 80s, a flight request came in during our family move from Big Bear California to Durango, Colorado. It was a request from Ann and Nancy Wilson to transport them from a TV appearance in Los Angeles, back to their home base in Seattle, WA.

At the time of the Heart request, I hadn't even unpacked a thing for my new home office location. I did have a phone line, but no computer or other office equipment was set up. LOL, our home had a 4-party [party - remember those?] line. I eventually moved my office to a downtown Durango location, since it was cheaper than obtaining a private home phone line. I was one of those with the first 'brick cell phone'. (Ha!)

No problem, I grabbed a piece of cardboard from a moving packing box and ripped the side from it for use as a large scratch pad.

This piece of cardboard was used to capture some essential details about the Wilson trip, which then turned out to be my complete project planning reference for this Heart endeavor.

https://flyingrocksbook.com/kwU
Credit given to YouTuber

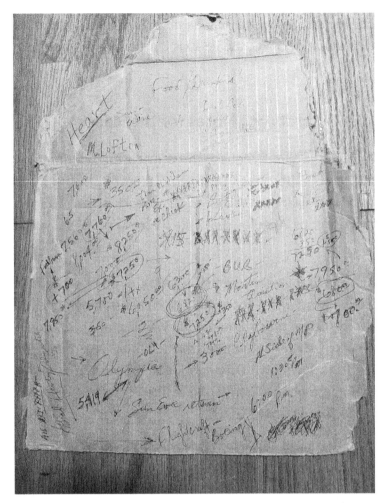

Heck, who needs a digital device when pen and paper (or a piece of cardboard, hehe) still serves the purpose? (sloppy but) LOL!

FLASH BACK 'Heart'... here are the girls and band jammin'-it-up in this 2013 (live) vid.

January 30, 2013: Barracuda - Proctors Theatre, Schenectady, NY

Credit is given to this YouTuber...
https://youtu.be/ooHBemmdASc?si=JQYs8ftPdfscUsrP

The Volcano Blew Again
Jimmy Buffett
West Coast Redux - 1983

The original Volcano album was recorded and released in '79. It was a slant referencing the AIR recording studio near the Soufriere Hills volcano on the island of Montserrat in the British West Indies. It also marked the second year of my thirteen-years as private flight consultation relationship with Jimmy and the Coral Reefer Band.

Volcano - Buffett Album

https://flyingrocksbook.com/hZQ

Ironically, Buffett revisited another volcano scene some years later. This time I was there for our flight experience.

Shortly after the 1980 Mount St. Helens eruption, JB had scheduled an acoustic tour of the Northwest. I secured a Beechcraft F-90 aircraft for such and took up the co-pilot position.

History of Beechcraft F-90 King Air

https://flyingrocksbook.com/o4Q

The Beechcraft KingAir F-90 was a rocket of a plane, with its upgraded Pratt and Whitney PT6A-135 engines, each delivering 750 shp (shaft horsepower) driving a pair of four-bladed propellers.

History of Pratt & Whitney engines

https://flyingrocksbook.com/kJo

Since it was an acoustic tour, only a few members of the Coral Reefer Band were on board, along with Jimmy and his road manager, Bobby. Without referencing their tour book, I believe we hit about six West Coast stops within a 10-day mini-tour.

USA West Coast Volcano Tour - Pilot/Author kneeling

At one part of this tour, we took off mid-day from our point of departure, Portland, OR. We decided to make a slight detour on our way to Jimmy's very next gig in Seattle.

Mt. St. Helens - Jimmy's Next Volcano

https://flyingrocksbook.com/ALE

St. Helens was still smoldering on this day, hence its top being blown off shortly beforehand. We had heard that private aircraft with proper transponder flight following could get a closer look in order to take a peek inside the bubbling blown-out lava pit.

This privilege was only available to very few private aircraft flying near St Helens. It was an excellent opportunity to view a historic event close [very close] from an aerial point of view.

After a few strategic radio calls to the Portland flight air traffic control center, we received our transponder code with further clearance to fly directly over the top of the volcano blow-out caldera. The transponder provides a dedicated signal of our location, speed, and altitude.

As we approached the volcano, we all were witnessing the smoldering cone in the very near distance. I suggested to Jimmy that he ride in the right (my co-pilot's) chair as we approached the flume. We began our descent to get the closest look possible.

Jimmy in my co-pilot's seat on the F-90 King Air

Upon our arrival, gazing from above into its bubbling smoky fissure, we dropped to just a couple hundred feet above ground level as we circled the volcanic rim.

Since our final descent was at such a very low altitude, I took the initiative to shut off the altitude awareness on our transponder. Even though I was sure the flight center couldn't tell how low we were, due to general ground interference. An additional cushion of selecting altitude reporting 'off' was another way to prevent any negative feedback from air traffic control. Even though, I figured they knew our approximate altitude. It didn't really matter since no other aircraft were in the vicinity of our volcano visit. (hehe)

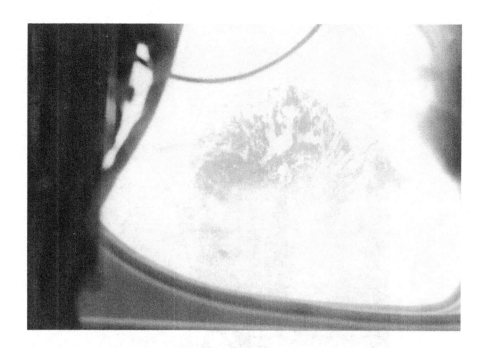

Looking into the Volcano from Buffet's side

What a Trip!

We were amongst the very few on this planet who had been able to look deep down inside a very recent volcanic eruption from an aircraft above. It was still doing a fair amount of huffin' and puffin'!

Very cool!

Our volcano experience was never recognized much beyond our inner circle of airplane passengers, as it isn't mentioned in places like Wiki. It was hence named the King Kong Mount St. Helens Volcano Tour.

OK, I'm calling it a redux of the earlier Montserrat Volcano Album.

Interior of the King Air F-90

Our first child, Fawn, was born just a few months before this tour. At that time our family lived in Big Bear Lake (Southern California). Young kids grow fast when you are on the road for just a couple of weeks. For sure, parents get this! BTW, Jimmy's daughter, Savannah, was born just a few years earlier.

https://www.savannahbuffett.com

Again, this story is not to confuse why Jimmy created the song, "Where do we go when the volcano blows?" In his book, he references such in the documentary, "Under The Volcano", in Montserrat'.

Under The Volcano - Documentary Trailer

https://flyingrocksbook.com/zWB

I'd be remiss if I didn't (also) include a quick story about our flight screw-up on this West Coast Volcano acoustic tour with Jimmy, which turned out OK, but oh boy...

You see, one of the last legs of this mini-tour had us fly from Seattle, just after the aforementioned Volcano viewing venture, to Spokane WA.

I know that someday I'll get shit from some pilots out there regarding this mishap, but at my age, it has long passed without harm to anyone at that time.

We were on a VFR (visual flight rules) flight that afternoon, albeit with flight following from air traffic control. It was a bit hazy in the Spokane region. Our destination airport was Felts Field just Northeast of downtown Spokane.

Whenever we arranged for airport landings, it was usually the closest airport to the gig or the hotel, that could accommodate our aircraft. Many times it wasn't a commercial airport, but a smaller but capable private landing port with facilities to handle our aircraft parking requirements.

As we approached Spokane, both the captain and I called out to each other for a visual verification of the airport. Only one problem, we called out seeing the runway for Spokane Regional, not Felts Field.

We continued our visual accent toward that airport, about ready to change our frequency to the tower to report, when the flight following air controller came on the radio and said, "Beechcraft N###, are you sure you see Felts Field, we have you descending toward Regional instead?"

Oh crap, we looked at each other and double-checked the coordinates of Regional, and sure enough, with the haze in the valley limiting our forward visual reference, we had indeed lined up at the wrong airport. The airports weren't that far apart from each other...

Oh Shit, mud on our face!

We weren't in any immediate danger since it was a very slow day for VFR air activity. Yet, not having flown in this valley before, we acknowledged the flight following their radio call and requested an immediate re-direct to Felts.

Never made that mistake ever again (LOL).

Finally, after landing, we secured ourselves at the proper parking facility.

Luckily for us pilots, it was a day that Jimmy was a tad hungover. He didn't give a hoot about our slight slip-up, since he just wanted to get to his hotel room ASAP for some rest before the show that eve.

Original Facebook Thread Regarding This Story

https://flyingrocksbook.com/OvJ

Author with Jimmy Buffett - Volcano Acoustic Tour

Jimmy in Seattle on the Volcano West Coast Tour

Doobie Brothers
Reunion Tour 1987

In the 50s through the late '70s, I grew up in the Altadena/Pasadena area of the Los Angeles, California basin, prior to my eventual migration to the So Cal mountains. While living there I mostly hung out at Brackett Airport in La Verne, California.

I spent most of my time in the '60s and '70s commuting back and forth between Altadena and LaVerne. My commute went by the old (original) Irwindale raceway where I had the opportunity to spend a fair amount of time with street car racing machines.

Brackett was where I obtained my solo and private pilot's licenses, including my tail-dragger endorsement in a Cessna-170. It was the main airport where for many years I also provided aircraft maintenance and inspections for two flying schools, Brackett Air Service and Jenny's Flying. At that time I obtained an aircraft airframe and powerplant (A&P) license, along with an Inspector Authorization (IA) certificate, allowing me to work on and inspect for flight any aircraft on the field.

Tail-wheel (dragger) endorsement

https://flyingrocksbook.com/HtG

I also, found myself obtaining my commercial license and a certified flight instructors rating (CFI) at Brackett airport. I subsequently provided flight lessons to a good amount of fledgling aviators.

Brackett Field So. Cal.

https://flyingrocksbook.com/U5O

There were numerous airports in the LA and Orange County basin where I ventured into, using many of the small aircraft I had access to...

Airports including the likes of (to name a few)... Chino, Ontario, Rialto, Big Bear, Riverside, Palomar, Catalina Island, Corona, Long Beach, Santa Ana, Palm Springs, Torrance, El Monte, Santa Monica, Burbank, Apple Valley, Van Nuys, etc. My aviation buddies and I hung out at a bunch of these airports in those days. Brackett was mostly my usual home base.

Chino Airport was one of the airports I ventured into. It was pretty much in the middle of cow country. Back then (and if you know the area) parts of the LA basin still had portions (mostly toward the Riverside region) devoted to farming, including milking cows, orange groves, et. al. Of course now it's currently built up with houses, condos, and commercial stuff.

Every airport in the Los Angeles area has its unique quality. Heck, even most of the desert airports for that matter just the other side of the LA basin mountain ranges offered some fun and unusual airplane flying excursions.

Chino airport, not unlike the other LA basin landing strips, retained a thick haze otherwise known as 'smog'! (smoke and haze). In the '60s and '70s, it was thick as shit... Thick! There would be times that even though you would be only a mile away from the local mountains, you couldn't see them!

The area surrounding Chino airport would additionally and occasionally reak of cow manure, since it was located smack dab in the middle of milking cow farm territory.

Back then and under those low (smog) visibility conditions pilots were required to fly under what is termed, special federal aviation visual flight rules (Special VFR). It required a special clearance to fly in the smog (aka soup) to remain safe distances from other aircraft within the airport environment.

Remember, we're talking about the '60s and '70s when Google (GPS) maps and the smartphone never existed. You had to rely on what was then called, steam gauges, relying on VORs, DMEs, and ILS indications to get you around your air routes. And hand-held paper-folding maps.

Older aircraft typically feature analog gauges, often referred to as "steam gauges," which include mechanical instruments like the airspeed indicator, altimeter, and attitude indicator. These gauges provide essential flight information through physical dials and needles.

steam gauges

In contrast, modern digital cockpits, known as "glass cockpits," use advanced digital displays to present flight data. These systems integrate multiple functions into large LCD screens, offering enhanced situational awareness, and easier readability, which reduces pilot workload.

glass cockpit

A pilot's pet peeve... The idea that a pilot climbs into a cockpit and watches a computer do all the flying is a bit unreal. There are routing changes, communications issues, navigational issues, monitoring engine performance, systems gauges, along with fuel burn. There's always some task going on. Pilots might not have their hands on the flight controls as often as they did years ago with upgraded autopilot, but they are still flying and managing every aspect of the aircraft's flight.

Back in the 1970s smog conditions in the Los Angeles Basin would be anywhere from a couple thousand feet thick, rising to as high as 7000 feet on some hot summer afternoons. And as I mentioned, you couldn't see more than a thousand feet in front of you on many days! It was ugly, nasty shit.

Many of my flight visits to Chino airport included aircraft maintenance and inspection work for a buddy/associate who ran a flight training service center. The same guy that I rebuilt an engine for on one of his training aircraft. We shortly thereafter broke it in by flying from the West Coast to Boston (where his family was) and back. Good trip! But that's another story... The engine did well, BTW.

Chino airport also housed some special and interesting pockets of curious aircraft parked on its ramp and snuggled within its numerous hangars.

Most trips to Chino were simply an excuse to fly into this airport to enjoy the best biscuits and gravy in the LA area at Flo's airport cafe. Also to otherwise gaze inside hangars filled with early pre and post-WWII aircraft, including an array of P-51s and many other unusual war and early-era air transport birds.

Chino was similar to Brackett Field, in that it was a small airport that didn't have extensive security, which you'd find at major airliner/commercial airports. The best part about hanging out at smaller airstrips is the fellowship of flying chatter. Along with the ability to walk around and peek into covey holes, where hidden aircraft gems await your gaze. Enjoyment without being hassled by what has now become a total joke (lmao,) ala, TSA (fgs!). Some pockets of these smaller airports remain, thank goodness!

Parked on the ramp at Chino Airport were the two large touring aircraft. They were used to transport the Doobie Brothers... The DC-3, named the Crewbie-Liner, and their Martin 404, known as the Doobie-Liner. Both aircraft were large vintage-type ex-airliners, with big round (radial) piston engines.

Radial Engines - eg., Pratt & Whitney

https://flyingrocksbook.com/13S

The dude at the time who managed and flew the Doobie Bros for years in the Crewbie and Doobie Liners was usually noodling about these aircraft. Especially just before a Doobies tour, readying these air-ships with repairs and updates.

One day while hanging out at Chino I remembered the existing flight crew members for the Doobies were making ready the Crewbie and Doobie Liners for Doobie's next tour outing.

I happened to know one of the Doobie's newest flight (co-pilot) recruits who was being checked out in the Crewbie-Liner (their

DC-3). After a short pre-flight conversation I was asked if I wanted to tag along and take a ride in the Crewbieliner, while the check ride was being conducted... "Of course!," I answered (in the most affirmative way).

We spent the better part of the afternoon flying locally and doing a lot of pattern work. It was great to just hang out and observe the training in the DC-3, remembering how docile the aircraft seemed. As a tail-wheel pilot myself, I appreciated the skills that the check pilot was exhibiting. I almost had the opportunity to sit behind the wheel that day, but the check ride took a little longer than expected, and we needed to get the DC-3 back to its stable for some post-flight work.

Little did I realize at that time that I would eventually have the chance (a decade later) to provide private aircraft consultation in support of the 1987 Doobie Brothers reunion tour. You never know what awaits just around the corner in the future, eh?

Fast forward about 10 years... Living in the mountains just above the LA Basin, in Big Bear, California, I spent the 80s and early 90s huddled down in my unfinished attic office space. I also spent some time at my other escape biz (office) location at the local Big Bear City airport, just down the street from our house. I further created and operated a Piper Aircraft dealership there for some local investors.

One day while reviewing one of my entertainment industry periodicals, which provided info regarding all upcoming entertainer tour announcements, I noticed that the Doobie Brothers announced that they were securing their final (well, final at that time - lol) reunion tour.

As you may know, the Doobie Bros. would continue touring well into the next century. The same as many bands that declared their last tour, only to continue for many tours thereafter.

I assumed they would take their Doobie and Crewbie liners for this recently announced tour. Yet, knowing the birds they used back in the Chino airport days were rather old and probably should have been retired.

Then I received a call from a booking agent who got wind of all my existing aviation experience, having flown many rock stars by that time. He asked if I heard that the Doobie Bros were doing a reunion tour. "Yes, just finished reading about their tour announcement," was my response.

The agent went on to state that the Doobie Bros aircraft operator had sold their older Crewbie and Doobie Liner aircraft. The band was now in the market to lease or charter a plane to handle this farewell tour.

Curiously I checked further, making sure that I wasn't stepping on an associate's foot, eg., the original Crewbie/Doobie Liners operator and chief pilot from Chino Airport.

During a certain time frame of many years in this industry (up until the early 90s) all of us private aircraft flight consultants were very much aware of which band's flight arrangements were handled by whom. We tended to respect those known providers. Flight brokers were indeed competitive on bands that were free to bid on, but respect nonetheless for bands that had been arranged for flight by certain aircraft consultants.

In this instance, once I discovered that the Doobie Brothers were open for bid and fair game without stepping on toes... It was 'game-on' baby!

China Grove - Live

https://flyingrocksbook.com/b7K

Viscount

Nowadays, hence the introduction of charter aircraft reference directories and online search engines, the research to locate available aircraft and crew became much easier, yet it made the competition crazy ridiculous. Back then, the manual labor was intense to locate the best existing available ships for tours. It was a big word-of-mouth industry in those days.

Once I secured the Doobie Brothers management lead from this original booking agent, and with their tour itinerary in hand, I hit the telephone hard. Digging for available aircraft. It was a semi-short tour. It required some special investigation to locate the right aircraft in the correct part of the country to be competitive in pricing.

Tracking down aircraft for tours took a bit of not only research but a decent amount of negotiating, especially in the days that allowed for legal FAA (Federal Aviation Administration) regulations (FARs) part 91D leasing on a short-term basis.

The trick to getting the appropriate aircraft for a touring gig was to not only find a certified airship at the time, you also needed to secure the best pilots for the trip. There would be times when an aircraft was available for a tour only to find out that no certified and current pilots with decent experience were available to subcontract. The aircraft used for my larger tours always required 2 pilots up front.

It could be a pain in the ass to coordinate all the elements. Many times I'd be pulling my hair out tracking down all of the components to secure touring projects. Playing phone tag much of the time. Again, back then, no reference guides, and for sure the Internet didn't exist.

The timing was everything in the business of securing proper aircraft for short-term entertainment tours. We're talking big aircraft here, not your everyday small jets that were more plentiful. Only a handful of large, 20-passenger executive-style seating, aircraft were available in the entire country.

I had told the Doobie's agent that I had the perfect aircraft in mind. But honestly, at the time I knew of only a few leads for aircraft and pilots, but had no idea if any of these contacts were going to synchronize. However, I was determined to secure this tour.

Diving into my leads one learns to search under every stone for available airplanes and supporting crew members. Inquiries, without divulging the touring band's name.

Once you give up the name or give a hint of the band you're looking to book into an airplane, every broker or aircraft operator in the world emerges to take it away from you. OK, I did mention earlier about the respect between brokers, but the industry did have its share of ruthless scavengers.

All of my phone calls paid off. I was able to score on a corporate interior Viscount Aircraft that had a certified crew available for the dates of the Doobies tour... Bingo!

Viscount Flight Deck

Doobie Brothers Reunion Tour 1987 was now in the bag, baby!... Short but sweet memories!

To quote Wikipedia...

"The reformation of the Doobie Brothers was not intentional. On a personal quest for a worthy cause and after conquering his drug addiction, Knudsen became active in the Vietnam Veterans Aid Foundation. In early 1987, he persuaded 11 Doobie alumni to join him for a concert to benefit veterans' causes. Answering the call were Tom Johnston, Pat Simmons, Jeff Baxter, John McFee, John Hartman, Michael Hossack, Chet McCracken, Michael McDonald, Cornelius Bumpus, Bobby LaKind and Tiran Porter. There were no surplus bass players as Weeks had other commitments.

They soon discovered that tickets were in great demand, so the concert quickly evolved into a 12-city tour that began on May 21, 1987, in San Diego. The third concert, held at the Hollywood Bowl, was reportedly the venue's fastest sell-out since the Beatles had played there just over 20 years earlier.

The band performed selections from every album using a wide variety of instrumentation that they could not have previously duplicated onstage without the expanded lineup. Baxter and McFee played pedal steel and violin, respectively, during "Black Water" and "Steamer Lane Breakdown". "Without You" featured four drummers and four lead guitarists. Producer Ted Templeman played percussion and LaKind sometimes played Knudsen's drum set while Knudsen went to the front of the stage to join the chorus.

The tour culminated (sans McDonald, McFee and Knudsen) at the Glasnost-inspired July 4 "Peace Concert" in Moscow, with Bonnie Raitt, James Taylor, and Santana sharing the bill. Excerpts appearing later that year on the Showtime cable network included a performance of "China Grove".

Memorabilia Patch

The Original DoobieLiner - credit Wiki

Itinerary

- https://www.setlist.fm/setlist/the-doobie-brothers/1987/calaveras-county-fairgrounds-angels-camp-ca-33cc6489.html June 21, 1987 **Jun 21** 1987
- https://www.setlist.fm/setlist/the-doobie-brothers/1987/calaveras-county-fairgrounds-angels-camp-ca-2bcc648a.html June 20, 1987 **Jun 20** 1987
- https://www.setlist.fm/setlist/the-doobie-brothers/1987/tacoma-dome-tacoma-wa-43c38f6b.html May 30, 1987 **May 30** 1987
- https://www.setlist.fm/setlist/the-doobie-brothers/1987/portland-memorial-coliseum-portland-or-23cc648b.html May 29, 1987 **May 29** 1987
- https://www.setlist.fm/setlist/the-doobie-brothers/1987/mcnichols-sports-arena-denver-co-3bcc6494.html May 27, 1987 **May 27** 1987
- https://www.setlist.fm/setlist/the-doobie-brothers/1987/shoreline-amphitheatre-mountain-view-ca-bc289fa.html May 25, 1987 **May 25** 1987
- https://www.setlist.fm/setlist/the-doobie-brothers/1987/aladdin-theater-las-vegas-nv-33cc6495.html May 24, 1987 **May 24** 1987
- https://www.setlist.fm/setlist/the-doobie-brothers/1987/hollywood-bowl-los-angeles-ca-2bcc6496.html May 23, 1987 **May 23** 1987
- https://www.setlist.fm/setlist/the-doobie-brothers/1987/shoreline-amphitheatre-mountain-view-ca-23cc6497.html May 22, 1987 **May 22** 1987

- https://www.setlist.fm/setlist/the-doobie-brothers/1987/san-diego-sports-arena-san-diego-ca-33d94c21.html May 21, 1987 **May 21** 1987

Many years later, after my family's move to Durango, Colorado, I met a lady named, Laurie. I learned that her ex-husband was the road manager of the Doobies. The same guy that was my point-man for this reunion tour. Synchronicity continued in Durango.

Los Angeles Times press release re: Doobie Brothers Reunion Tour

https://flyingrocksbook.com/M9w

BestClassicBands.com article re: Doobie Brothers Reunion Tour whereby a couple of its vids are also posted at the Flying Rocks book website... FlyingRocksBook.com

https://bestclassicbands.com/doobie-brothers-interview-2-2-166/

Rolling Stones

Steel Wheels Tour

In 1989 I arranged all of the personal USA tour flights for the Rolling Stones Steel Wheels Tour as their private aircraft transportation consultant.

Original Tour Book

I had the opportunity and arranged to fly the boys on their Steel Wheels North America tour in a Boeing 707/720 type edition aircraft. Ok, you might be thinking, a 707, isn't that old? This was in '89 mind you and this aircraft didn't have a ton of airtime regarding its use. It was only used as a corporate aircraft, which meant that the flying time on the aircraft was limited and was much less than that of an airliner. Less usage provided for a more reliable airship.

The Boeing with its military designation VC-137C, was also used during many presidents' tours as Air Force One from 1973 to 2001 (not this particular Stones ship, lol), including President Reagan's administration until '89. It now resides at the Reagan Library and Museum in California. Around 1991 the Boeing 747 aircraft took over Air Force One's duties.

Video History of the Boeing 707/720 aircraft

https://flyingrocksbook.com/pAe

A year later when the Rolling Stones opportunity arose, it hit me that this Boeing, with an executive interior, was one of the few aircraft available on the market that could handle such a large tour.

Only a handful of private aircraft consultants were vying for a crack at flying this Rolling Stones tour. I happened to come across this Boeing ship during an inspection in Houston of another aircraft a year before the RS tour. I remember seeing the Boeing airplane on the ramp adjacent to an aircraft I was inspecting. I inquired as to whom owned it. I learned that it was owned and operated by an oil company located in Houston.

Timing (I called it synchronicity) was a large portion of how the consultation biz worked during my time as a private aircraft consultant. With a contact lead in my hand, I promptly called the management company handling the Stones to let them know who

I was (and the experience I already had flying rock n' roll) and mentioned that I had the perfect aircraft for their tour. Some call it cold calling. Yet, since I had my chops for many years in the biz already, I considered it a warm call.

Boeing 707/720

This bird was converted from 120 commercial airline passenger seats to a 44-passenger corporate interior containing lounges, two staterooms, a bedroom, bathrooms, a galley capable of providing gourmet cuisine, and a working shower!

The existing aircraft brokers (like myself) had already started calling the Stones management office hence their media-released tour announcement. My competitors were seeking the Stones tour itinerary, yet none of them actually had an aircraft to offer them. I was the first and only with a real aircraft to show and bid against the Stones tour itinerary. I now had the edge... LOL!

I had sold my consulting services with the existing Boeing to the Stones office, before ever knowing of the aircraft's availability and securement thereof. It was, like many aviation flight consultations, a hat dance between communicating with the entertainment managers and the aircraft ownership entities at the same time. All timing baby!

Without having gone into details on what type of aircraft and its parked location, since the industry had a way of going around you once you divulged your sources, I immediately got the attention of the Stones management. This gave me the slight edge to go forth with the itinerary in hand to communicate with the aircraft owner to further engage in dialog to secure the plane for their tour.

I went to work contacting the aircraft owner, initiating an interest in flying a rock band. A good week of research and investigation into the Boeing's ownership. A phone call to the right contact leads me to a quick trip to Houston from my Durango Colorado home to further seal the deal.

It's kinda funny that securing a large aircraft like this Boeing 707 isn't much different than closing a deal for a smaller aircraft for charter. However, as with most of my earliest large aircraft securements, this Boeing was set up under Federal Aviation Regulation part 91D. Meaning, it was required to be a lease with sub-contracted flight crew members. More paperwork, but I had done it many times before with other larger ships.

While I was in Houston the Rolling Stones management was calling me almost daily to determine what type of aircraft was forthcoming and the bid for such. As with many large aircraft deals in the industry, you play a game of cat and mouse between the aircraft owners and the entertainment management. Most of the time all the pieces come together (albeit many pieces), other times it's a total train wreck that needs much more care and work to complete all of the elements.

In this case, once in Houston, the meeting with the aircraft owner went smoothly enough to have them sign an industry standard, non-disclosure agreement. I let them know that the client I was working with was the Rolling Stones I could then start the ball rolling on both sides.

First, I needed to secure a ballpark figure on what the aircraft owner wanted to lease the plane and its crew daily for the duration of the Stones tour. I already had their Steel Wheels tour itinerary from my earlier communique with the RS management office. Now, it was time to initiate a rough draft bid to test the fiduciary waters on both sides of the equation between the Stones and the Boeing owner. Inclusive of my commission to launch and support the complete tour.

Most of my tour bids to entertainment management companies tended to be delivered by firstly locating the best aircraft for the tour. Yet sometimes, I'd bid a tour out without even having an aircraft available or knowing where the plane was going to be sourced, simply because I knew the approximate cost of most makes and models of airplanes available, then later securing the aircraft directly with its operator/vendor.

Geographic location was generally the best course to consider as the airplane-related tour's itinerary. In this instance, the size of the aircraft (the Boeing) was paramount and its location didn't matter as much as knowing that the aircraft was my baby and the wholesale cost factors made it a viable solution for (in this touring instance) the Stones.

Once I got the non-circumvention/non-disclosure agreement secured with the aircraft ownership regarding the band they'd be touring, I was then free to further disclose more information to the Stones.

As a part of my non-circumvention contract outline, any calls directly or indirectly related to the use of this aircraft for the Rolling Stones had to first be referred to me as the main point of contact. I was now in control of an important half of the equation... the aircraft. The very hard to find, aircraft.

I knew once the word got out about this airplane and since this was one of the very few (like maybe 2) aircraft available for this RS Steel Wheels tour, every touring broker on the planet would be trying to undercut me and attempting a go around. It was an everyday issue I dealt with as a broker in the aircraft booking industry.

The next thing I knew the Stones tour itinerary was fitting rather well into the oil company's Boeing schedule and the aircraft owner was supplying me with a decent wholesale daily and flight hours quote. The initial cost figures I sent to the Stones, after my retail bump to the wholesale numbers, were received rather well. It was game on!

I was now getting calls from competitive brokers claiming that the industry scuttlebutt was that the Stones were looking to go with my airplane suggestion and pricing. But I knew better than to rely on industry gossip, as this could have turned against me if I didn't play cool and sit on my hands before the 100 percent 'go' signal from both the Stones and the aircraft operator. I was juggling cats and trusting I wasn't going to get scratched. Pending a solid flight contract signed by both sides.

Within a couple of weeks from the very first phone call I made to the Stones management office, I secured and sent an initial draft aircraft lease contract to the attorneys representing both sides.

From my first knowledge of the Steel Wheels tour to the start of the first itinerary leg pick-up point, it was only six weeks out! One thing about bidding for tours is they are going to start within a short time, whether you get the gig or not.

Boeing Interior

The Rolling Stones toured during the Thanksgiving holiday and I remember getting a call from the road/tour manager right before our Thanksgiving dinner.

My wife at that time (the mother of our two children) said; "don't answer it." But I knew better with a client on the road, I answered at all times of the day.

The Stones road manager wanted to remind me that Mick wanted the shower hot-water temp at exactly 137 degrees. Yep, that Boeing aircraft had a shower as a part of the interior layout.

I accommodated his request by contacting the service base the aircraft was parked, to make sure the H2O temperature would be on the mark for when the Stones showed up for departure that day. Yet, the band never used the shower but maybe once to see if it functioned during the tour legs. (LOL)

I do remember suggesting to the road manager that we were just about ready eat our Thanksgiving meal... and he, ever so quaintly remind me that; "We're English, we don't celebrate Thanksgiving!"... Made sense to me, as I eventually explained such to my wife. HA!

The lesson I learned from providing private aircraft transportation consultation for the largest of entertainers in the world was to keep a fairly low profile. In this instance, however, the Rolling Stones' 'tongue' plastered on the side of the aircraft (marketing) gave a clue. It was pretty obvious who was on the aircraft.

Credit Given to...
The Rolling Stones

https://flyingrocksbook.com/Mnb

There was one time I convinced the aircraft parking personnel at an airport location that required us to remain on the low-down. I mentioned that the tongue was an icon for a 'flag' of the foreign country that owned the aircraft. LOL!

Most of the time we couldn't hide the fact that the boys were on the plane. Fortunately, parking a private (air)ship from 'plane' sight (hehe) - away from prying eyes - comes easily enough with the territory of personal aircraft.

At the time, this tour was considered the most sophisticated planning and marketing ever attempted in large band outings. It turned out to be the most lucrative concert trek in the history of popular music.

My very rare RS Touring Jacket

Ships Passing In The Same Town

Van Halen / Hagar / VIII

https://flyingrocksbook.com/mEP

My earliest stomping ground (born and raised) was Altadena, California, a small town just above Pasadena, right up against the Southern California San Gabriel mountain foothills. Eddie, Alex, David, and Michael, would meet and create Van Halen near me.

Pasadena is the home of the Rose Bowl and its namesake New Year's Day Parade. The Rose Bowl parking lot was where I learned to drive a car. Mt. Wilson sits atop the San Gabriels. Just across the canyon to the west is the secretive Jet Propulsion Laboratory (JPL). Some very interesting places to hike around growing up in that area.

https://flyingrocksbook.com/zmZ
Credit given to the YouTuber

One of the Tour Books

A couple of years behind me, David Lee Roth, went to the same High School as I, John Muir. Alex and Eddie went to our rival football school across town, Pasadena High. We had our major football rivalry every year at the famous Pasadena Rose Bowl... called, the Turkey Tussle.

I also spent some time attending Pasadena City College (PCC) where apparently Michael Anthony and Eddie met. Here again, I didn't know any of the boys at that time... Even with myself spending a little time at the PCC radio station as a DJ, back when we played full album sides over the air (LOL), I never had the chance of running into the VH guys on campus.

Van Halen Facebook thread on PCC concerts...
https://www.facebook.com/grenoff/posts/10100605112097888

Even though the Van Halen band members all lived in the same town where I grew up, I never really thought much about their existence. I wouldn't actually brush into them until a couple of decades later as their personal private aircraft touring consultant.

I do, however, remember in my late teens driving by a couple of Van Halen's private home parties in Altadena. One eastward just down the block from our old original Altadena Library. They also had some big gatherings at their location in South Pasadena. At that time (around 1972) they were known early on as, Mammoth.

Van Halen's backyard parties were pretty massive. It was a great excuse at that time for the Pasadena police department to put to use their newest helicopters. Flying around these backyard jams, shining their spotlights down onto tons of stoned youth partygoers. I only drove by those parties, never in attendance, probably on my way to other parties (LOL), but I got the full feeling of the scene for sure. There were tons of local peeps!

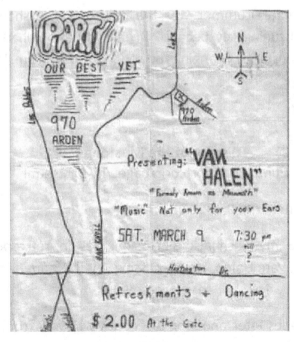

Back when Mammoth was transitioning to Van Halen I was in numerous youth rock bands myself... It was a great way to be a big shot at guitar playing and to pretend to impress girls!

At the time of this publication, I continue my band jammin' ways, albeit switching to playing drums in the 90s. This old man is averaging a gig every other week... Mostly private parties, weddings, and as an open mic drummer host. It keeps my limbs moving and it provides a few bucks on the side. (self-absorbed bio at the back of the book)

A bit off this topic but, one of my major influences in getting into playing the traps was my high school drum corp, aka, the Mighty John Muir Mustang Marching Band.

As of 2024, the Mighty Mustangs celebrated over 70 years of drum corp marching at John Muir (founded 1956, Pasadena, CA.) football games and at many New Year's Rose Parades. You might say that my school was way racially mixed (my senior graduation was '70) as I witnessed the original 60s Watts riots smoke rising from our campus viewpoint, and there's no doubt where this white boy found his early 'soul'!

To quote the head drummer of the mighty Mustangs: "The most important thing about the Muir drums was the tuning. He said that the Head Drummer was the only one that should have a drum head tuning key because if each drummer had one, they would be constantly changing the sound of their drum." LOL.

History of the Mustangs
http://muiralumnidrumcorp.org/pages/history.shtml

https://youtu.be/-k60ndPsoQE

OK, excuse my flashback digression. Yet in retrospect, that's where my Van Halen, ships passing in the same town, story developed.

A few decades later and long after moving away from Altadena, the phone rang at my humble Big Bear City attic office with the tour management on the horn for Van Halen, asking for some assistance with a quote for private air transportation for their upcoming tour.

I had been a private aircraft consultant for the touring industry for many years by that time, and my name was liquid in the entertainment and flying business.

When I received the phone call about the upcoming VH tour, Roth had left the band for his own trip, and it was the debut of the latest Van Halen line-up with their newest frontman, Sammy Hagar. Many called it the Van-Hagar years. IMHO, they were still Van Halen for sure!

At the time of that VH phone inquiry, it didn't hit me that it was a part of my high school brushes in life. I might now be consulting the private air transportation for my ex-stomping grounds band. Now one of the largest rock bands on the planet. Life has a way of delivering some cool and wacky circle-back spin-arounds!

Their tour manager, Scotty, requested that I secure an aircraft charter quote for their upcoming tour. After a month of negotiating with him, I subsequently arranged their private aircraft transportation in private planes for all of their Tours, 7-years after starting in the mid-nineties. Nice!

I (subjectively) loved the line-up with Sammy. He was a bad-ass rock singer and knew his way around the guitar.

Van Halen turned out to be one of my last entertainment groups having provided private aircraft touring consulting biz for over twenty years, just before I retired from the entertainment aircraft consultation biz. It was ironically around that same time after 9-11 (go figure!).

My consult with the band continued, right up to the disassembly of this Van Halen line-up (departure of Sammy) and the subsequent addition of Gary Cherone on vocals, via era VH-III.

Essentially, the last private aircraft I provided was until the very end of the (essential) VH era. Although they re-gathered with Roth for a short stint, until the unfortunate departure from this planet due to the illness of Eddie in 2020.

As you probably already know, they (the mix of VH talent) went on tour for a few dates where Sammy and David (aka: 'Sam & Dave' Tour) would switch off during sets. According to Sammy and other supportive articles, this reunion crashed and burned. Not the plane, but the tour! It happened early on due to band in-fighting, Subsequently, that was it for VH for a while.

Eddie's son, Wolfgang, picked up the bass duties and carried forward with some touring activities thereinafter. I hated to see Michael Anthony go but was very happy to see Sammy Hagar and him hooking up for subsequent work.

My Facebook thread: - (ed. Note, grab another news release citation re Eddie's passing)

https://www.facebook.com/MichaelLofton/posts/10222347932459901

Brown M&M's

Their now-infamous rider specified that a bowl of M&M's, with all of the brown M&M's removed, was to be placed in their dressing room. According to David Lee Roth, this was listed in the technical portion of the contract not because the band wanted to make capricious demands of the venue, but rather as a test of whether or not the contract had been thoroughly read and honored, as it contained other requirements involving legitimate safety concerns.

Brown M&M clip

https://flyingrocksbook.com/SHY

Backstage Chicago...

I was one of only a handful of individuals allowed backstage, it was a very quiet and secure scene. You wouldn't see any groupies before the show in their backstage area. It was off-limits to anyone except essential personnel. I met Eddie's wife Valerie and his son Wolfgang. He was maybe 8 years old then. I spoke briefly about airplanes with Eddie, Alex, and Sammy, before they hit the stage.

Van Halen was one of my last entertainment groups that I handled in my aviation consultation career. I pretty much checked out of the industry shortly after Sept 11, '01. Private aviation just wasn't as much fun after that unfortunate episode.

Anyway, I remembered VH's last flight home from the Mid-West back to Burbank California. It was an after the show (quick out) return home flight. I knew the air-route pattern would take the aircraft right over my house in Durango Colorado around 2 am. I had arranged for a Hawker Jet to handle this final flight leg.

At two in the morning during a quiet night outside of my Colorado home, I was sitting and waiting for the Hawker flyover. Since it was near the end of my aviation consultation biz, it seemed a fitting farewell to see the aircraft strobe lights and hear the sound of that Hawker flyover. Albeit, the craft was about 30,000 ft up, on that morning, the clear blackened sky allowed me to witness and enjoy its westward flight path.

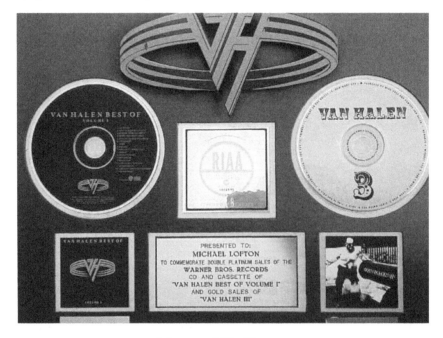

Memorabilia Plaque

some backstage passes

Van Halen connections to Pasadena CA.

https://flyingrocksbook.com/lsb

Guns N' Roses

The BFD, Use Your Illusion, Riot Tour

'Get in the Ring Mother F*cker'

A buddy of mine in the entertainment transportation business, Robert Skilton (may he forever RIP), handled many touring buses for high-level rock bands. He tipped me off to the Guns n' Roses, BFD Use Your Illusion, tour. Ultimately, it was later known as the Riot Tour.

I knew that once the word got out to the industry about Guns n' Roses hitting the road, everyone and their puppy would be bidding on their flight itinerary.

Again, the trick to securing rock tours in the [my] biz of aviation rock touring days, was to find the right aircraft first. Then immediately secure a non-circumvention agreement with the airline operator, giving first rights to negotiate the plane with the band management.

Then once band management had an interest in the plane, it was handed over to the road manager to obtain their flight legs and touring (itinerary) dates. From then on, it was who could research, get to, and secure the right available aircraft that could handle the gig first. Along with the most aggressive price structure, without sacrificing safety and profits.

In this instance, I had already worked with this big-name aircraft operator in Los Angeles who had an executive Boeing 727. I knew it would fit the bill for this Gn'R tour. Besides, it was the only large (airline type) with corporate seating aircraft available during those itinerary flight dates. The other aircraft operators were already booked with other tours, preventing their availability for this tour.

I also remember knowing that once the tour was on, I needed to bear down and get to work! Including a few visits with the aircraft vendor in Los Angeles. Initially creating agreements back and forth with legal.

After many weeks of continued negotiations, everything was falling into place. I had secured the documentation agreements between the attorneys for the Gn'R management and the contracted corporate airline company. As a corporate flight consultant, I'm always in the middle of any of these negotiations as a buffer between the client and vendor, and to keep the project on the rails (sort of speak).

Road management flight itinerary details, and money transfer arrangements with their accountants, had been accomplished.

Finally came the time to launch the BFD (Big Fuckin' Deal)/Riot Tour.

During the launch and immediately thereafter all went rather smoothly. My daily contact with the Gn'R road manager and my airline aircraft vendor continued to support a successful tour.

The weather was decent throughout the flight schedules and almost all the touring legs went without a hitch. Everybody seemed happy. We were nearing the end of another successful rock tour.

Then, the shit hit the fan!

It was late the evening of July 2nd, 1991 when I got a call from the airplane vendor's corporate executive. He was on the road (but not on the band's airplane) following the tour for a couple of concert dates.

They were in St. Louis at this point of the tour.

He starts off our conversation with, "Michael, we've got a big problem on the road tonight. Not sure if you've already caught wind of this but the shit has hit the fan, and we'll need some brilliant ideas to get us the hell out of dodge without any hassles!"

Perplexed, I further inquired as to what happened...

On that late July evening at the Riverport Amphitheater in Maryland Heights, Missouri, just outside of St. Louis, during a performance of "Rocket Queen", lead singer, Axl Rose discovered that a fan was filming (yep oh my, videotaping) the show with a camera.

Guns n' Roses Riot Night Documentary

https://flyingrocksbook.com/2cn

Now mind you, this was just before the smart-phone craze and cameras were a no-no to many bands. Can you imagine not getting free advertisement airtime these days? Omg! Well, you could also realize that online streaming didn't exist then. Of course, nowadays (most all) bands don't worry about folk recording their ass.

After asking the venue's security to take the camera away, Rose decided to take it upon himself to jump into the audience and tackle the fan. And a smackdown ensued.

Ha!... can you imagine today, requesting that you turn off your camera during a concert?... [everyone in the venue would go... WTF-FU -Huh!?].

It was 1991, which was of course before our cellphone phenomenon, and filming with a live video feed at a gig for most bands was taboo for most live acts. Albeit, bands like the Grateful Dead had learned to encourage it well before the digital age. Mmm.

Amazing what just a decade meant [means] when it comes to the digital world regarding capturing images and passing them on.

Axle had a heated confrontation with that camera fan, including physically assaulting him. After being pulled out of the audience by members of his stage crew, Rose said, "Well, thanks to the lame-ass security, I'm going home!", threw his microphone to the ground, and stormed off the stage.

With the free marketing exposure concepts available, you'd think the Gn'R band, even back then, would have taken advantage of such free marketing... But whatever, that was then.

The concert-going crowd didn't take too friendly to Axle's early departure from the concert that evening. For sure angry, many began to #riot. Literal chaos!

Dozens of people were injured along with the destruction of a shitload of physical objects. Fixed chairs at the venue were pulled up and tossed on stage. And it appeared that some of the stage gear, amps, and drums, were damaged.

My flight crew members (the captain, co-pilot, and stewardess) along with a couple of the airline corporate bigwigs, were just 4 rows back center stage, and they viewed the whole spectacle firsthand right in front of their eyes. Flying beer cans, chairs, shoes, and babies (well ok, most everything but babies).

The crew members and corporate wigs figured their best resort before the SWAT team's arrival was to exit and get the fuck outta there, pronto!

Soon after the ruckus, that very same night a discussion with the

Guns n' Roses road and production managers ensued to determine a plan of how we would handle the flight departure from St. Louis..

Since the press already knew where their airplane was parked, they had already dispatched reporters to the airport to be near any sort of band departure. And, now the police were involved and wanted to do a bit of interrogation with Mr Axle and the band management.

Many ideas were kicked around to handle a simple departure from St. Louis. Finally, I suggested that we consider sending in another 'diversion' aircraft early the next morning, to another airport in the area, other than the location where our existing tour aircraft already resided.

We made darn sure that the press and everyone at the original private aircraft parking facility knew about this new (dummy) aircraft that was going to land at the other airport to retrieve some Guns n' Roses crew members. This way we would pull the attention away from our main touring aircraft parked at the other airport on the other side of St. Louis. The main band members had already headed out the night after the riot in Limos to the next stop in Chicago.

My suggestion about the dummy airplane was given the go-ahead by Gn'R management.

After spending a decent amount of last-minute time calling around for another aircraft that was not only close enough but big enough to pull off this one-day fill-in airplane scheme, I managed to secure another semi-large corporate aircraft, which was a Gulfstream II airplane. I arranged to have it ferried to our diversion St. Louis airport, away from the existing parked touring craft. I did mention that we might be flying some of the sound and lighting crew members for the band, and I would assign the airport for their next flight once they secured the airplane in place that very next day.

The reason I didn't tell the airport parking facility personnel it was the Gn'R band instead of the sound and lighting crew for the band, was that I wanted to stay somewhat clean about the whole matter. I mean, I was in the middle of a get-a-way plan, albeit not an illegal one, but it felt like it at the time... (hehe). And I wanted the pilots from the diversion plane to announce that they were there to pick up some stage crew members from the Guns n' Roses group, to make sure that the alternative airport FBO (Fixed Based Operator) thought the same.

All the while, we made sure to have the St. Louis press and I could only imagine a detective or two were alerted to the news that the plane for Gn'R was to be at the other airport for a late morning departure.

The next day, after our diversion aircraft arrived and had secured itself at the alternative airport parking ramp, the press was awaiting at that airport. I was finally able to have the flight crew of the original band airplane secure a departure from St. Louis to the next destination.

And we blew out-of-dodge somewhat unnoticed. Plan pulled-off!

It felt like we just conquered a country by mutiny baby... LOL!

Once airborne, my next move was to contact the diversion airplane to let them know that the Gn'R stage crew had decided to go instead on the tour bus with the rest of the stage crew. Since they were already paid to position the airplane, I released them to return to their place of operation without any passenger flight.

After that concert episode, Rose was wanted by the local law enforcement for inciting the riot. However, the police were unable to arrest him until almost a year later, as the band went overseas to continue their tour.

In the meantime and after the charges were filed against Rose, a judge ruled that he did not directly incite the riot. Ha, must have indeed been that fuckn' dude in the crowd with a camera. Oh-man!

The bummer for me at that time was the fact that a portion of the tour was canceled hence this episode, along with a damn decent bit of my income for this gig! But the experience and story... Can't beat it!

Interestingly enough, the sub-title of this tour was... 'Get in the Ring Mother Fucker'. [LOL – Go Figure!]

226

Cocaine and Wine Stains in the Chrysler Airplane?
Grateful Dead

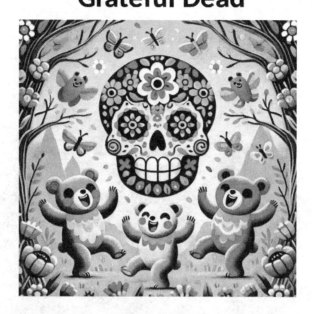

On a different occasion, while working with another upper-level corporate aviation charter department, another interesting event took place on a Dead tour. This time it was on a chartered aircraft owned and operated by the (original, back in the day of Lee Iaccoca) Chrysler Automotive Corporation out of Michigan.

Many corps, as I'd assume many today, would register their aircraft under Federal Aviation Regulation Part 135 (aircraft charter guideline rules) to sub-let out their craft to earn side income as a chartered plane. The additional tax incentive was also very apparent.

As you no doubt have noticed so far, I don't really mention most living individuals or corporations that still exist that I've worked with, except given to the bands I've flown. Only because they are a public entity and nothing in this book is going to take them down, FGS! In this instance, however, Chrysler was bought out many eons ago and it became another entity altogether... Fair game!

It was another Grateful 'mini-tour'. I called them mini-tours because they were generally less than a couple of weeks long in duration. Just a few stops, since many times they played several dates in the same city. They'd even sometimes go out for a few concert dates at each location and then return home after the gigs until their very next outing.

Production Crew Tour Jacket (a rare one)

The legs of this particular mini-tour were the mid-west. Around the states of Illinois and Michigan.

On many occasions, the Dead would travel with girlfriends, wives, and their children, along with some personal assistants. As such, the corporate aircraft I contracted would need to accommodate strollers, infant cribs, bicycles, and the like.

It was always interesting to hear the responses from many of my corporate aircraft sub-contractors that it seemed unusual to have kids fly around the country on a rock concert tour. However, most found it a pleasant surprise that the Dead were family-oriented and as such traveled with their families!

With most large corporation flight departments, I usually went through the same sort of shit as I did with the Banks Won't Fly The Dead chapter. A corporate flight booking representative saying (such as), "You're representing rock n' roll bands? We're not sure if we want to work with you" would be their usual blab.

I learned to live with such push-back since I eventually became rather good at closing deals with this standard resistance response. As I earned the reputation as being real, most Corp flight departments would take my calls and cooperate by providing me with an immediate contract price for most all of my itinerary requests.

In this instance, I locked down one of Chrysler's Grumman Gulfstream II Corporate planes for the Dead's mini-tour. Like most ships, she was a beauty with a comfortable interior.

Gulfstream II Aircraft

Flying Rocks Book .com

One of Grateful's interiors - without wine stains - LOL

https://flyingrocksbook.com/kaO
(G-1159 Gulfstream II Aircraft referenced by Wiki)

Once on the road, it all seemed to be going swimmingly! Well, that was until the very last leg of the tour. The final leg happened to be the same destination landing point as Chrysler's home aviation base in Michigan.

Sitting in my humble attic office in Big Bear City, CA. my phone rings. It's the VP of operations for Chrysler. Note: not the VP of the aviation department, it's the VP of Chrysler's overall operations!

He goes, "Mr. Lofton, we have a problem and this is not sitting well with us!"

"OK," my return voice continues, "What seems to be the issue?"

Whenever I received calls like this, my first and foremost concern was if there were any safety issues or accidents. So, right from the start of our conversation, my further comment was, "Is everyone safe? Was there any sort of accident I need to be aware of? Anyone hurt?" The VP Ops said, "No accident, and I appreciate your thought regarding such, but we definitely have a problem."

After assuring myself that no episode regarding an accident occurred, I was now in a thank goodness, pretty full-relief mode.

The (head) VP continues, "You see when the airplane arrived back at our stable [aviation talk for hanger or home base] we noticed cocaine on one of the tables and wine stains on the white couch in the back! I'm about ready to call the authorities on your band and for sure you're getting charged big time for the clean-up!" He also goes on to say, "And to top that off, Mr. Iaccoca is set to use the aircraft today... We'll need to address this situation immediately!"

After taking a deep breath and somewhat appreciating his raised voice I agreed that we'd pay for any clean-up of the airplane that the band was responsible for. I did my best to have him reconsider his reference to calling the authorities, whomever they might have been. He mentioned that he would get back to me within the hour to determine the final resolution, once his clean-up crew had finished with their post-flight chores.

Standing by... As I recall, I went down my funky attic fold-out office stairway and fetched a cup of hot tea in anticipation of my next round with this corporate uppity-up.

In the meantime, I was somewhat perplexed. I could see a wine stain, but all of my bands were very discerning about any drug-type paraphernalia exposed (or being left) after flights. Hardly ever happened, especially (believe it or not) with the Grateful Dead.

Within an hour of my original conversation with the head VP at Chrysler, he returned the promised call.

By this time I figured, whatever, the band was safely on the ground and that was the most important ingredient in my book regarding any flight. I was prepared for the post-flight reprimand from Iaccoca's dude.

The VP opens our conversation with, "Michael, I owe you and your Grateful Dead band an enormous and sincere apology." I go, "OK?"

He goes on to say, "I originally received what now has appeared to be an initial seat-of-the-pants, misleading, response from my ground cleaning crew." He continued, "They thought that since this was a rock band, they were presumptuous with their reporting of the cocaine and wine."

"You see, Michael" he continues, "Our stewardess this trip had already gone to our flight planning lounge right after the arrival of the aircraft to handle post-flight duties. When she returned to the airplane to meet up with our cleaning crew, she had to explain what really was left on the table and couch, and now I know for sure that it was not cocaine and wine."

Remember, the Stew worked for Chrysler and came with our aircraft charter contract.

Now, I'm thinking to myself while listening to his voice, at least the authorities aren't going to be involved. Yet, being very curious about our final outcome, I asked, "So tell me (Mr. VP) what happened?"

The VP once again led with an apology and went on to explain, "Well, apparently your band travels with young kids?" My immediate answer was, "Yes, they do from time to time." He goes, "Well, it looks as though a diaper was changed and instead of cocaine, it was baby powder." (OMG!)

I'm now fully thinking to myself that this is getting good! LOL, really good!

LOL

Continuing, the VP says, "And, it also appears that the wine stain was our stewardess accidentally pouring 'grape juice' in a baby bottle while spilling some."

OMG, man... I wanted to jump through the phone and slap this VP silly, but figured his humble pie was plenty enough and I enjoyed every minute of it!

The funny part at the very end was when the VP was virtually on his knees urging me to consider using Chrysler Aviation whenever it worked for me in the near future. Laughed to myself, thanked him for his apology, and mentioned I'd consider their flight department for future touring needs as they arise.

After hanging up from our conversation, I immediately poured myself a glass of good dry Cabernet Sauvignon... Spilled a little bit of vino on purpose later that eve!... Heck, I might have even found myself some baby powder... LOL!

Another rock n' roll flight story in the can!

One of Jerry's last gigs

I was at one of Jerry's last gigs at Soldier Field in Chicago. Quite the experience with a towed car situation. Story further to be told at the Flying Rocks Book Blog (one day).

Buffett Meets Skynyrd Inflight?

Mystery Unforeseen
- Conclusion from Chapter One -

"I looked out my right side and witnessed sparks flying out from the front of our right-hand #2 engine... Lots of bright, flying sparks! WTF!?" The lights in the flight deck started to flicker and once again the autopilot clicked off... And again the co-captain called out, "I've got the ship!" This time we both acknowledge that we had a more serious situation at hand.

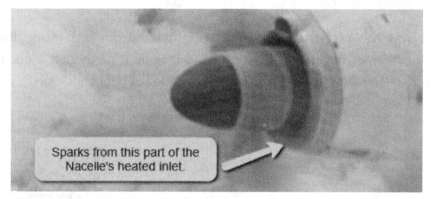

Sparks from this part of the Nacelle's heated inlet.

The whole episode took place within minutes, however, when you're honed in on the situation at hand it feels like a lifetime!

It was indeed decision time, since if it were an engine turbine blade rubbing condition we couldn't risk further engine damage, as well as a possible in-flight fire, by any means. Yet, we hadn't experienced any vibration which would have indicated an engine rubbing condition.

Even though we had continuous stable engine gauge read-out conditions, we needed to make a decision soon.

I called out to the captain... "Let me take one more good hard look and we'll make our final decision momentarily." he responded, "Your call, Michael."

This time I really visually honed-in on that engine and concentrated on where the immense amount of sparks emitted. Since up to this point in our flight, the sparks never provided a definitive answer to this discrepancy.

In this instance, I further noticed that the sparks weren't coming from inside the engine itself, but from the engine inlet perimeter, its nacelle. It was from the inside portion of the anti-ice ring surrounding the air intake of our turboprop engine.

The engine anti-ice nacelle uses a high electrical current to heat this area to prevent ice build-up at higher altitudes and/or under freezing flight conditions.

Two of the high voltage heating element wires were obviously shorting out, creating our fireworks show.

It was the fact that the sparks originated from just inside the engine inlet nacelle that initially had it appear as though it could have been from an internal spinning blade rubbing condition.

Anti Icing Engine Nacelle Systems

https://flyingrocksbook.com/n0L

During my confirmation that it indeed was a nacelle anti-icing issue, the co-captain once again asked, " Michael, do we have a starboard engine shutdown situation?"

This time, my response to the captain was definitive, "No,

Negative!"

At that moment I simply and immediately reached up to the appropriate panel on the flight deck's ceiling switches and announced to the captain that I was, "selecting the appropriate RH Engine anti-ice switch to the off position."

After verbal confirmation from Captain Bill, the correct anti-icing switch to the starboard engine inlet, I clicked it off.

Voila, no more sparks!!!

With the simple click of that switch, all that wacky sparkler display ceased, and all of our on-board indicators, including stability in the flight and cabin lights, returned to normal, immediately.

And all at once, there was some peace and calm on the flight deck.

Original Cheeseburger Fairchild F27 Cockpit

We continued to monitor our flight instruments as we continued to manually fly the aircraft. We hadn't settled in just yet.

After a couple of minutes, Captain Bill says, "Well, that was an interesting experience, wouldn't you agree?"... with my follow-up, "No shit it was!"

I went on to explain in further detail to the captain this scenario from my point of view... We celebrated with a sigh of relief from our recent flight deck tension.

After further bringing back on-line our 'B' (right-hand starboard engine 'B') electric bus, we once again secured the autopilot with no further issues and proceeded along to our planned landing destination.

Bobby, JB's road manager comes back up to the cockpit and we have some time to explain the scenario. He goes, "Damn, sounds like you guys had your hands full for a while." "No shit" was my simple response.

We were able to secure a lower altitude in warmer outside air temperatures. Our flight conditions were clearer skies that prevailed for the remainder of our trip. We noted the anti-ice squawk in our flight logs.

All this excitement took place within just a very few short minutes, yet at the time (as mentioned) it seemed to go on for quite a while. But as you can imagine, some circumstances can just seem longer than the actual occurrence you've experienced.

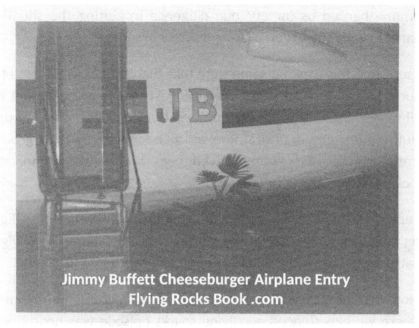

F27 Cheeseburger Airplane Main Entry

Once we landed at our final destination, I was outside by the right engine, looking up at the intake along with Buffett. I was explaining to Jimmy what had happened and all the steps we took on the flight deck during this crazy event.

The best I could tell was, I went to explain to Jimmy, we must have picked-up some Foreign Object Damage (FOD) from our original point of departure runway... No doubt, something on the ground like a small rock pebble (or something like that) was lifted from the ground by our propeller wind (aka prop wash) and caused some damage to the engine anti-ice nacelle.

Foreign Object Damage (FOD)

https://flyingrocksbook.com/y1h

The FOD provided just enough damage to show its true discrepancy at altitude, where the outside air pressure change launched the episode of sparkage!

Jimmy thanked us for our due diligence in getting the situation handled with professionalism and safety in mind.

I sure that this was the same time that thanked all of the band for our times on tour together over the past couple of years and we all wished each other happy journeys. Hugs and kisses and all that stuff! Buffett and the Coral Reefers then loaded into their ground transportation and Jimmy stayed near me on the ramp, still looking at the engine inlet.

Captain William came around the front of the aircraft with a flight sectional map. I had requested it to look over our recent flight path. Maps back then were paper, not digital read-outs... hehe.

I looked down at the map and confirmed with Jimmy that the area where we experienced our flying sparks episode was nearly over the town of, Gillsburg, Mississippi. Where indeed, Skynyrd and, even close to where, Jim Croce had crashed.

"Yikes, OMG, No Shit?!" was my remark. Jimmy goes, "Well isn't that interesting!"

Dumbfounded at that time, we couldn't tell if this was just a coincidence, or was it an explicit warning that maybe we were being fucked with by the spirits of LS, with a gentle nudge from the Skynyrd folk saying...

"Hello, Dudes - greetings from the other side. We were just kinda fuckin' with you just a little bit... Continue to Rock On Your Way Brothers!"

Since it was one of our very last legs, after those late 70s years of touring with Jimmy in the Cheeseburger F-27, it seemed only appropriate for something strange like this to happen as a farewell and remembrance to personally flying Jimmy and the Coral Reefers.

After being the personal Pilot for JB and the CRB during '78 & '79, I then went on to handle all of their personal private aircraft touring arrangements for another ten years. Ending my time with Jimmy and crew in 1991.

I remembered the very first day we picked the band up in the Cheeseburger airplane a couple of years earlier, and was reminded that Jimmy's entourage resembled the Lynaryd Skynyrd group, right down to their two girls' backup singers.

A very timely tribute reminder to Lynaryd Skynyrd and Rock n' Roll! Mmm, it was so sweet, and it will forever be!

Almost Famous In-Flight Disruption
Please - It's a Parody Scene!

https://flyingrocksbook.com/xNA

I'm sure you may already know this but, the Almost Famous plane scene shows a parody with way stupid (on purpose) pilots. In real life, passengers would have been warned well in advance about rough weather. But parody is a parody, fgs!... And no, the back of the Cheeseburger plane didn't experience the same this eve. LOL. Note that the type of aircraft represented appears to be a Beech 18 (re: Otis Redding and Jim Croce)

Interestingly enough, on September 20, 1973, at the height of his popularity and the day before the lead single to his fifth album, *I Got a Name* was released, Jim Croce and five others died in a plane crash, trying to depart in a Beechcraft-18 from Natchitoches Regional Airport, Louisiana.

Well, the interesting thing about this was not only did I remember this incident years before I took up flying entertainers in private aircraft, but Croce's crash site happened within a couple hundred miles from Skynard's mishap! Close enough to call the whole thing a strangely double-related coincidence. Yet, are there coincidences, or were they predetermined synchronistic events? I'm going with the latter!

Bubbles Up!

Revisiting The Cheeseburger Airplane
A Death In Puerto Rico

Two Decades Later the Cheeseburger Airplane laid to rest

Whatever Happened to the Cheeseburger F27 Airplane?

Re-visiting the old gal 20HE in Puerto Rico...

Years after flying Jimmy Buffett and at one point in my flight career, I provided expert aviation consultant input for court hearings. One such investigation took me to Puerto Rico. Ironically, I was inspecting an F27. While at the airport I looked across the tarmac and to my shock and surprise there she was, the old Cheeseburger airplane. She wasn't looking so good.

The ex-Cheeseburger plane had been turned into a commercial entity. The original executive interior had been replaced with all forward-facing airline seating. It was obvious that it had not flown for many moons. The side forward cargo door was wide open.

As I approached the bird, I started flashing back in a big way. The earlier days we spent on this plane provided incredible memories. I started shedding a few tears in reflection. I took a peek inside. She just wasn't the same lovely flying machine. The JB letters aft the rear airstair were painted over. The interior was in shambles.

It was a damn shame the Cheeseburger plane met its fate, yet I was in appreciation to had the opportunity to at least bid a fond adieu one more time. RIP Cheeseburger!

20HE. I just looked it up in the FAA Registry and noticed the tail number has been de-registered, whereby the F27 N20HE was indeed its last assigned ship.

Facebook locator for this Jimmy Buffett thread:
https://www.facebook.com/MichaelLofton/posts/10208023182230098

Facebook image with Jimmy and Bobby on their Gulfstream 1

https://flyingrocksbook.com/gAh

Mountain Aire '78

https://flyingrocksbook.com/OzE

1978 Coral Reefer Band:

Jimmy Buffett – Vocals, Guitar
Barry Chance – Guitar
Harry Dailey – Bass, Background Vocals
Deborah McColl – Background Vocals
Katy Moffatt - Background Vocals ('78 tours)
Greg "Fingers" Taylor – Harmonica, Background Vocals
Jay Spell – Piano
Michael Utley – Keyboard/Organ
Kenneth Buttrey – Drums

Michael
The Cheeseburger Tour wouldn't have been anywhere near as successful with you guys and the plane. It's a love with from a Beech-18 and a pilot who wanted to double as a piano player. Thanks for being Prost
Jimmy Buffett

I also placed many touring acts in the Gulfstream 1
Including Jimmy Buffett

Author with Jimmy and Bobby - Flying Rocks Book .com

Example Gulfstream interior

Liner notes credit Cheeseburger airplane and pilots

The Deaths of Jimmy and The Coral Reefers...

Many have passed (as of this date late 2024)
Jimmy Buffett, Harry Daily, Fingers Taylor, Jay Spell, Kenneth Buttrey, and Barry Chance.

Side note...
Mac McAnally's history and how it also related to CRB.
Great and very deep interview...
https://youtu.be/FkEIO60NthI?si=UswsU9RSg-hGGC3J

Florida's Historic A1A Officially Named After Buffett

https://flyingrocksbook.com/xtc

Refer to the book...
A Good Life All The Way, by: Jimmy Buffett

JB and the Original Coral Reefers here...

https://flyingrocksbook.com/eb1

Conclusion, Bio, and Acknowledgments

Back to the 70s in my 70s

I had already turned 70 years old by the time I finally got around to finishing the first edition of this book. Call it being lazy to complete, yet, over many years I continued to reflect upon stories and references that support the content in Flying Rocks and its supporting Blog, FlyingRocksBook.com

I grew up in Altadena California as an offspring of my parents, John and Pauline. My three brothers, Ron, Steve, and Bob, often played Wiffleball in our driveway. I was a skateboarder, had a paper route, a Little League pitcher (my Dad was the coach), raised homing pigeons, a vanner, a surfer, and a street car racer.

In retrospect, the last quarter of my life seemed a safe and essential part of writing a memoir (kind of a dossier). I'm admitting upfront that I'm not a seasoned writer, so you'll no doubt discover a few twists and turns in my grammatical approach. I did however go through a ton of edits just to get to this point.

I might have written this particular book similarly to the one you'd write for yourself. You know, one that not only captures a snapshot of your personal past experiences as they reflect upon the world, where some might relate or at least find interesting, but even more so, as a way to document one's experiences to pass them along to your offspring, and their offspring, as a way to provide an encapsulated reference for your family tree.

In my case, I'm sharing snapshots of the wacky backstage production world of music entertainment touring in private aircraft.

My fascination with flying and music started back when I was in elementary school, playing guitar with my first band, the Turning Point. Later in high school, I was with another band, called; Green Bread (not moldy bread but, green, like money - LOL).

My first rock band '66 - The Turning Point

aka: The Liverpool Boys of Altadena CA. USA
(Me on the left with my big ears - My mom created the suits!)

https://www.facebook.com/photo.php?fbid=10200617317888118

Other bands names along the way included; Pointz Beyond, Furniture, Foam, Turtle Spit, Interface, and Stoned Wasp. (Might have forgotten a few, hehe). Lots of great players.

Vikings dance to one of the groups at the battle of the bands contest on January 25 in the Blair gym.

2/2/68

'Green Bread' Wins Competition at Dance

The Green Bread from John Muir High School was awarded first prize in Blair's Battle of the Bands Dance.

The Green Bread, along with the Moving Sounds from PHS, the Atomic Duck from PHS, the Mendus Blues Band from Muir, the American Tragedy from PCC, PHS, and Blair, and the Pacific Electric Blues Band, battled for four hours in the Blair gym, January 25.

The dance, which had been announced for the preceding week over KRLA, was open to everyone. Students from PHS, Muir, Blair, and other schools came to dance and vote for their favorite band. Each group player 40 minutes while spectators watched and danced. Upon entering the gym each person was give na yellow slip that entitled him to one vote for the band of his choice.

The Green Bread, voted the winner of the contest, was awarded $100. The group has been playing together for only a month and a half. The American Tragedy was voted the second place winner and awarded $40.

The Battle of the Bands Dance was sponsored by the Junior Class and grossed over $400. The profits will be used to pay for the Junior-Senior Prom.

Randy Best, last semester's Junior Class president, stated, "In my opinion the dance was a success, but more Blair students should have supported it because it was mostly attended by students from other schools."

This is the second year the Vikings have held a Battle of the Bands.

Green Bread Wins Battle of The Bands - High School Contest

Sidebar: (not verified but) My long-ago bandmate, Michael Porter, suggested that the (pre) Van Halen band, Mamouth, was possibly at this same battle of the bands that night, where our band won. Indeed for the record, Alex and Eddie went to my rival cross-town High School, while at the same time, Roth attended my local, Pasadena So. Cal. John Muir High.

Yet, flying and inspecting aircraft took hold and became my main paying, professional career, from early college till 2010.

My first solo airplane flight took place in southern California at Bracket Field Airport in La Verne, CA in Sept of 1970. I had just turned 18. My solo was in a tail-wheel Cessna 170A airplane, which I spent most of my earliest days learning to fly and earning my private pilot's license in the same year, along with a tail-wheel endorsement.

First Solo Airplane - Cessna 170

https://flyingrocksbook.com/1wF

While building flight time on the side, I was also attending an aviation technology school (Jr. College) in Glendale, CA, where I earned my Airframe and Powerplant (A & P) technician's license. And, within a few years thereafter I secured my Inspectors' Authorization (IA) certificate. I could then legally inspect and work on most aircraft.

Subsequently, I maintained two flight schools, including Jenny's Flying at Brackett Field in Southern California. It was owned by one of the first WASP women. WASP (Women Airforce Service Pilots) test-flew and delivered WWII military aircraft all over the world.

I rebuilt crashed planes (called basketcases). Fabricated and inspected numerous experimental ships. Constructed small private airplane hangars in Durango, Colorado, and Los Alamos, New Mexico.

The technical side of my aviation adventures was no doubt inspired by my dad being a hands-on carpenter. Along with my first biz experience at the age of 12, running a bike repair shop out of our residential neighborhood garage in Altadena, California. My interest in music was inspired by my Mom being an artist.

I eventually obtained additional flight hours to become a commercially rated pilot, along with a certified flight instructor

(CFI) rating. Most of my flight hours happened while trading aircraft maintenance and inspections on aircraft that my customers owned, in exchange for the use of their aircraft. Taught flying lessons. Was a Safety Counselor for the Federal Aviation Administration. Also, did a bit of aircraft repossessions for banks on the side (ha).

Most of my fellow flight buddies were dead set on an airline career. Me, being the black sheep of our group, I wasn't so sure about my flying pilgrimage. Eventually, I steered toward the corporate aviation route.

While at Brackett Airport in Southern California in the early 70s, I met many wonderful pilots and flight-related associates. Had the opportunity to fly small aircraft all over the United States, Canada, and Mexico.

On any given day I never knew where a flight might lead. Many times my aviation comrades would just call out an airport to do lunch. Or, maybe even a quick hop over the mountains to the desert to land on a strip of uninhabited earth. These ventures were indeed spontaneous and adventurous!

Reminding myself that during those times I didn't have but a few nickels to rub together. Trading flight times with my clients for maintaining and inspecting their aircraft was my inroad to aviation.

For example, one time after rebuilding an engine for a customer it was recommended that we break that engine in with a flight across the country. So, within days I had packed some clothes and the next venture was numerous flights in that small aircraft from So. Cal. to Boston and back. The engine did good! (thank goodness! hehe)

One day while hanging out at the airport, an associate asked if I could assist him in setting up an aircraft charter company to fly fishermen to Baja Mexico from Southern CA. I jumped at the opportunity. Being only 19 years old at that time the adventure intrigued me.

I was later asked to fly to San Francisco to inspect a twin-engine Cessna 414 aircraft to handle those Baja trips. It was owned by the person who started the EST training system (remember those guys?) in Northern California.

Example of the C-414

Indeed it was an unusual airplane and a very capable cra*. It sported a wacky paint scheme, being all green in color with gold stripes. I eventually maintained and flew many fishermen to Baja over the next couple of years in that C-414 bird.

Then the Bands Came...

Shortly thereafter, around the mid-seventies, I managed to stumble into flying rock bands on the road... Literally stumbled into it!

I first found myself in Burbank (Hollywood) airport sub-contracting as an occasional flight support and maintenance crew personnel for an outfit called, Go Enterprises.

The airplane used for these entertainers from Go was the Viscount. A British-designed craft, which was very popular in the music touring industry. If you haven't already, you'll discover artists in this book who used the Viscount aircraft for their tours.

In the flight consultation biz, I had a few corporate aircraft choices to present to my flying entertainment clients. Most all offerings fell under the Federal Aviation Regulations (FAR) - Charter Part 135 or Lease Part 91D. On rare occasions, some purchased their own aircraft. Nowadays, flight options include... Charter Cards, Membership Access, Per Seat/Shared Charter,

Fractional Ownership, and Purchase Leaseback Management, are included within FAR parts, 91, 135, 121 and 125.

My earliest years flying rock was from a small mountain town in Southern California, called, Crestline. Within a couple of years, I had moved up the mountain to a place called, Big Bear City. With the assistance of local business investors, we started a Piper Aircraft Dealership at the local airport, while I continued to build my flying consultation career flying major music entertainers.

Author with his Cessna 421 in 1978 (a past life!)

I married in Big Bear and our home was within walking distance of the Big Bear City Airport. I had an office at the airport, yet, my main consulting biz activities took place in my humble home (pull down the stairs from the ceiling) attic office. (hehe!). Many great memories of flying in and out of Big Bear, including flights with many friends and associates, including uncle Dougie.

In those early years, I jumped out of an aircraft (4 total jumps - whoopie!) in the summer of 1972 using a double 'L' canopy by the name of 'Alice'. (yeah, like with boats, most parachutists named their chutes). Maybe you've done this yourself? Let me know over at Flying Rocks Blog or its Facebook location.

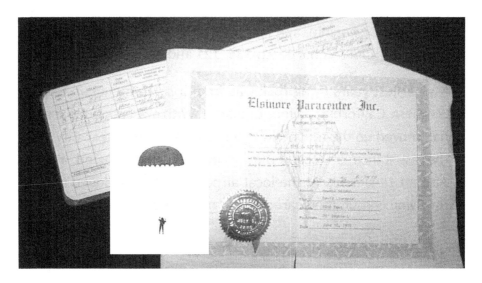

Eventually, our family moved to Durango, Colorado, where I was the first to build a few aircraft hangars at the local La-Plata County airport. I continued to provide entertainment aircraft touring services.

As synchronicity would have it, my Ex-wife's (Sunshine) first cousin is Sam Feldman, who owns (and still does I believe) the largest Canadian management company of many major music entertainers. We spent a bit of time with Sam. He came to our wedding and we went to his. I never flew any of his Canadian accounts. Synchronicity nonetheless. My ex-sister-in-law, Elaine, worked for Sam and his associate, Bruce Allen. No doubt she has some stories to tell. Yet, like myself, many that will remain secret. (hehe)

I did have a bit of publishing experience by creating a few (award-winning) glossy aviation magazine releases in early 2000/01 along with co-publisher and producer, Paul Dutcher, including our sales department head, Rick... called, Air, The Aviation Journal.

Thereafter, I climbed into a marketing career. I am currently (at the onset of this publication) an online and brick-and-mortar, new-age SEO content conversion strategist. I also get to play a bit of golf.

Picked up a few awards for flying entertainers...

An 'ex'-Catholic alter boy, I continue (so far) to play in bands for small clubs as a semi-professional, having switched from guitar to drums in the early 90s. Many years as a radio DJ for College station KDUR in Durango, Colorado. Currently, MacGyver activities around the house along with my SEOing consultations.

I wanted to play drums with Spinal Tap, but they had a requirement that you could not have any next of kin to qualify.
LOL!

Spinal Tap Drummers

https://flyingrocksbook.com/7Ny

With the Grandkids at a gig (cir. First edition 2024)
Brooklyn, Cole, and Xander

Acknowledgments

Design and Edit Contribution

Ethan & Wynd Lofton - Cover design and Website edits
Tamara Essie Crocker - Copy edits

I made enough money to buy Miami,
　… but I pissed it away so fast
　… never meant to last !
JB
(however, his lasted!)

Fly & Rock On!
FlyingRocksBook.com

Made in the USA
Monee, IL
27 May 2025

18284753R00155